SPECTRUM MATHS

▼ NUMBER ▲

Teacher's

3

Dave Kirkby

Collins Educational

Author
Dave Kirkby

Series and cover design
Sylvia Tate

Design
Perry Tate Design

Cover artwork
Katty McMurray

Artwork
Roy Mitchell, Wendy Sinclair, Lisa Williams

The author and publishers gratefully acknowledge permission to reproduce an extract from *The Trouble with Ben* by Barrie Wade and Maggie Moore (Collins Educational, 1996), © Barrie Wade and Maggie Moore 1996.

Published by Collins Educational
An imprint of HarperCollins*Publishers* Ltd
77–85 Fulham Palace Road
Hammersmith
London W6 8JB

Telephone ordering and information: 0870 0100 441

The HarperCollins website address is: www.**fireandwater**.com

First published 1999

ISBN 0 00 312747 8

British Library Cataloguing in Publication Data
A catalogue record for this book is available from the British Library.

Printed in Great Britain by Martins the Printers, Berwick-upon-Tweed

Contents

Correlation to the Framework

Spectrum activities for Year 3 objectives

Key objectives are bold.

Summary of objectives: Year 3		Activities in Teacher's Book 3
NUMBERS AND THE NUMBER SYSTEM		
Counting, properties of numbers and number sequences	Count larger collections by grouping them: for example, in tens, then other numbers.	
	Describe and extend number sequences: **count on or back in tens or hundreds, starting from any two- or three-digit number.** count on or back in twos starting from any two-digit number, and recognise odd and even numbers to at least 100; count on in steps of 3, 4 or 5 from any small number to at least 50, then back again.	3, 35 34
	Recognise two-digit and three-digit multiples of 2, 5 or 10, and three-digit multiples of 50 and 100.	1, 16, 29
Place value and ordering	**Read and write whole numbers to at least 1000** in figures and words.	Opportunities in most activities
	Know what each digit represents, and partition three-digit numbers into a multiple of 100, a multiple of tens and ones (HTU).	1, 3, 18, 39
	Read and begin to write the vocabulary of comparing and ordering numbers, including ordinal numbers to at least 100. Compare two given three-digit numbers, say which is more or less, and give a number which lies between them.	1, 3, 13, 18, 24, 35, 39 3, 18, 39
	Say the number that is 1, 10 or 100 more or less than any given two- or three-digit number.	1, 39
	Order whole numbers to at least 1000, and position them on a number line.	1
Estimating and rounding	Read and begin to write the vocabulary of estimation and approximation. Give a sensible estimate of up to about 100 objects.	9, 20, 31
	Round any two-digit number to the nearest 10 and any three-digit number to the nearest 100.	18
Fractions	**Recognise unit fractions such as $\frac{1}{2}$, $\frac{1}{3}$, $\frac{1}{4}$, $\frac{1}{5}$, $\frac{1}{10}$... and use them to find fractions of shapes and numbers.** Begin to recognise simple fractions that are several parts of a whole, such as $\frac{3}{4}$, $\frac{2}{3}$ or $\frac{3}{10}$. Begin to recognise simple equivalent fractions: for example, five tenths and one half, five fifths and one whole. Compare familiar fractions: for example, know that on the number line one half lies between one quarter and three quarters. Estimate a simple fraction.	10, 25 10 10
CALCULATIONS		
Understanding addition and subtraction	Extend understanding of the operations of addition and subtraction, read and begin to write the related vocabulary, and continue to recognise that addition can be done in any order. Use the +, − and = signs.	2, 6, 7, 8, 12, 14, 16, 19, 21, 24, 30, 32, 33, 34
	Extend understanding that more than two numbers can be added; add three or four single-digit numbers mentally, or three or four two-digit numbers with the help of apparatus or pencil and paper.	2, 6, 7, 11, 16, 17, 22, 28, 30, 40
	Extend understanding that subtraction is the inverse of addition.	15, 19, 33

Summary of objectives: Year 3		Activities in Teacher's Book 3
Rapid recall of addition and subtraction facts	**Know by heart:** **all addition and subtraction facts for each number to 20;** all pairs of multiples of 100 with a total of 1000 (e.g. 300 + 700). Derive quickly: all pairs of multiples of 5 with a total of 100 (e.g. 35 + 65).	2, 6, 7, 8, 12, 13, 14, 15, 19, 21, 22, 24, 25, 28, 30, 33, 34, 37
Mental calculation strategies (+ and –)	Use knowledge that addition can be done in any order to do mental calculations more efficiently. For example, put the larger number first and count on; add three or four small numbers by putting the largest number first and/or finding pairs totalling 9, 10 or 11; partition into '5 and a bit' when adding 6, 7, 8 or 9 (e.g. 47 + 8 = 45 + 2 + 5 + 3 = 50 + 5 = 55); partition into tens and units, then recombine (e.g. 34 + 53 = 30 + 50 + 4 + 3).	32 6, 7, 15, 17, 28, 30 11, 15 32
	Find a small difference by counting up from the smaller to the larger number (e.g. 102 – 97).	8, 19, 24
	Identify near doubles, using doubles already known (e.g. 80 + 81).	
	Add and subtract mentally a 'near multiple of 10' to or from a two-digit number... by adding or subtracting 10, 20, 30... and adjusting.	11, 15
	Use patterns of similar calculations.	
	Say or write a subtraction statement corresponding to a given addition statement, and vice versa.	15, 19
	Use known number facts and place value to add/subtract mentally.	8, 32
	Bridge through a multiple of 10, then adjust.	32
Pencil and paper procedures (+ and –)	Use informal pencil and paper methods to support, record or explain HTU ± TU, HTU ± HTU. Begin to use column addition and subtraction for HTU ± TU where the calculation cannot easily be done mentally.	
Understanding multiplication and division	Understand multiplication as repeated addition. Read and begin to write the related vocabulary. Extend understanding that multiplication can be done in any order.	4, 26, 29 26
	Understand division as grouping (repeated subtraction) or sharing. Read and begin to write the related vocabulary. **Recognise that division is the inverse of multiplication,** and that halving is the inverse of doubling.	29, 33, 36
	Begin to find remainders after simple division.	36
	Round up or down after division, depending on the context.	
Rapid recall of multiplication and division facts	**Know by heart:** **multiplication facts for the 2, 5 and 10 times-tables.** Begin to know the 3 and 4 times-tables.	4, 11, 25, 26, 29, 35, 40 4, 11, 25, 26, 29, 35
	Derive quickly: division facts corresponding to the 2, 5 and 10 times-tables; doubles of all whole numbers to at least 20 (e.g. 17 + 17 or 17 × 2); doubles of multiples of 5 to 100 (e.g. 75 × 2, 90 × 2); doubles of multiples of 50 to 500 (e.g. 450 × 2); and all the corresponding halves (e.g. 36 ÷ 2, half of 130, 900 ÷ 2).	29, 36 11, 25, 40 11, 40 25

Correlation to the Framework

Summary of objectives: Year 3		Activities in Teacher's Book 3
Mental calculation strategies (× and ÷)	To multiply by 10/100, shift the digits one/two places to the left.	
	Use doubling or halving, starting from known facts (e.g. 8 × 4 is double 4 × 4).	
	Say or write a division statement corresponding to a given multiplication statement.	36
	Use known number facts and place value to carry out mentally simple multiplications and divisions.	29
Checking results of calculations	Check subtraction with addition, halving with doubling and division with multiplication.	25, 33
	Repeat addition or multiplication in a different order.	25
	Check with an equivalent calculation.	25
SOLVING PROBLEMS		
Making decisions	**Choose and use appropriate operations (including multiplication and division) to solve word problems,** and appropriate ways of calculating: mental, mental with jottings, pencil and paper.	25, and opportunities in most main activities or 'developments'
Reasoning about numbers or shapes	Solve mathematical problems or puzzles, recognise simple patterns and relationships, generalise and predict. Suggest extensions by asking 'What if...?'	1, 2, 4, 12, 13, 14, 15, 17, 22, 26, 30, 32, 34, 35, 37, 40
	Investigate a general statement about familiar numbers or shapes by finding examples that satisfy it.	1, 4
	Explain methods and reasoning orally and, where appropriate, in writing.	3, 13, 18, 39
Problems involving 'real life', money and measures	Solve word problems involving numbers in 'real life' on money and measures, using one or more steps, including finding totals and giving change, and working out which coins to pay. Explain how the problem was solved.	16
	Recognise all coins and notes. **Understand and use £.p notation** (for example, know that £3.06 is £3 and 6p).	16
HANDLING DATA		
Organising and using data	**Solve a given problem by organising and interpreting numerical data in simple lists, tables and graphs,** for example:	5
	simple frequency tables;	9, 20, 23, 31, 38
	pictograms – symbol representing two units; bar charts – intervals labelled in ones then twos;	9, 20, 23, 31, 38
	Venn and Carroll diagrams (one criterion).	

Summary of objectives: Year 3		Activities in Teacher's Book 3
MEASURES, SHAPE AND SPACE		
Measures	Read and begin to write the vocabulary related to length, mass and capacity.	27
	Measure and compare using standard units (km, m, cm, kg, g, l, ml), including using a ruler to draw and measure lines to the nearest half centimetre.	27
	Know the relationships between kilometres and metres, metres and centimetres, kilograms and grams, litres and millilitres.	
	Begin to use decimal notation for metres and centimetres.	27
	Suggest suitable units and measuring equipment to estimate or measure length, mass or capacity.	
	Read scales to the nearest division (labelled or unlabelled).	
	Record estimates and measurements to the nearest whole or half unit (e.g. 'about 3.5 kg'), or in mixed units (e.g. '3 m and 20 cm').	27
	Read and begin to write the vocabulary related to time. **Use units of time and know the relationships between them (second, minute, hour, day, week, month, year).** Suggest suitable units to estimate or measure time.	
	Use a calendar. Read the time to 5 minutes on an analogue clock and a 12-hour digital clock, and use the notation 9:40.	

Spectrum Maths – Number does not cover 'shape and space' objectives.

Introduction

The National Numeracy Strategy

The National Numeracy Project developed the Framework for Teaching Mathematics in the drive to improve standards in numeracy. The Framework comprises a set of yearly teaching programmes for National Curriculum mathematics, providing primary teachers with guidance for teaching the programmes of study at Key Stages 1 and 2. Specific yearly objectives are grouped into five strands, three linked to number – 'Numbers and the number system', 'Calculations', 'Solving problems' – as well as two strands linked to 'Handling data' and 'Measures, shape and space'. Key objectives for each of the strands are highlighted and supplementary examples show what pupils should be taught to do by the end of the year.

The Framework's approach is based on daily mathematics lessons, focusing on **direct teaching** of the whole class and groups, on mental calculation and on controlled differentiation. The structure of the daily maths lesson reflects these principles:

▲ whole-class introduction, with an emphasis on oral
   work and mental calculation   (5–10 minutes)
▲ main teaching activity, which includes teaching input
   and pupil activities with the whole class, groups, pairs
   or individuals   (30–40 minutes)
▲ plenary session to conclude: work with the whole
   class to identify misconceptions and progress, summarise
   key facts, discuss next steps and set homework   (10–15 minutes)

Mathematics 5–14

In Scotland, the National Guidelines on Mathematics 5–14 provide the rationale and structure for the teaching of mathematics. The Guidelines offer five two-yearly levels of attainment A to E. The levels are divided into four attainment outcomes – 'Problem-solving and enquiry'; 'Information handling'; 'Number, money and measurement'; 'Shape, position and movement' – which give primary teachers a structure for organising appropriate programmes of study. Each outcome is subdivided into strands and targets which offer more detailed advice on the learning objectives. For many of the targets, examples are included to illustrate the depth of study and to suggest possible contexts for learning.

There has been an increasing focus on the importance of number, and on the effective development of strategies for mental calculation in particular. *Spectrum Maths – Number* can help teachers to improve their pupils' number skills by:

▲ offering clear learning objectives which can be referenced to the Guidelines;
▲ providing notes and activities to support direct, interactive teaching;
▲ indicating a structure for lessons;
▲ encouraging investigative learning and suggesting developments and extensions;
▲ highlighting key strategies for the effective development of mental skills;
▲ emphasising the use of simple practical equipment, games and puzzles.

Spectrum Maths – Number: an overview

Following the enormous success of the original series, *Spectrum Maths – Number* has been completely revised to match the requirements of the Framework for Teaching Mathematics and Maths 5–14, covering number, data handling and measures. This resource for Years 1–6 (P2–P7) provides teacher-led activities for the daily maths lesson. Please see the correlation chart on pp. 4–7 for details of the specific objectives covered at Year 3.

Teacher's Books

There are six Teacher's Books in the series – one per year – offering a broad spectrum of activities for the daily maths lesson. Each lesson features:

▲ clear objectives, referenced to the Framework;
▲ suggestions for whole-class introductions and relevant mental strategies;
▲ key mathematical vocabulary;
▲ notes for the main lesson, a photocopiable activity or game to support group/pair work, and answers for quick reference;
▲ developments – ideas for adapting the activity for differentiation and extension;
▲ a list of materials needed;
▲ reference to the related individual activity in the Workbook or Pupil Book.

Every Teacher's Book also includes generic photocopy masters at the back, plus answers to all activities from the relevant Workbooks or Pupil Book.

Workbooks and Pupil Books

Two Workbooks for each of Years 1–2 (P2–P3) and one Pupil Book for each of Years 3–6 (P4–P7) provide individual practice linked to the main teaching activities. Each lesson in the Teacher's Book is cross-referenced to at least one page in the Workbook or Pupil Book and shares the same activity number. The pupil materials reinforce the main activities and are ideal for homework.

Planning and teaching with Spectrum Maths – Number

Spectrum Maths – Number is a flexible resource; it can be used alongside any main maths scheme to provide comprehensive number coverage. A correlation chart in each Teacher's Book (see pp. 4–7) provides an at-a-glance reference to *Spectrum* activities that meet the Framework's number, data handling and measures objectives for that year.

All the activities have been written to aid interactive, direct teaching of the whole class, groups and pairs. The series also promotes other key teaching points from the Framework, including:

▲ ensuring that number facts and mental calculation methods are thoroughly established;
▲ emphasising the correct mathematical vocabulary and notation;
▲ extending lessons through activities that take place outside the maths lesson or at home.

Using Spectrum Maths – Number

Teacher's notes

▲ objectives and key vocabulary from the Framework

▲ whole-class introductions focusing on oral work (often includes mental strategies)

▲ notes for the main teaching activity (with answers where relevant)

▲ development ideas for differentiation and extension

▲ materials needed for the main activity and developments

---

6 Activity

Elephant totals

Key vocabulary

total
larger/
smaller

Objectives

Understanding addition and subtraction
▲ Extend understanding of addition and recognise that it can be done in any order
▲ Add three single-digit numbers mentally

Rapid recall of addition facts
▲ Recall addition facts for numbers to 20

Mental calculation strategies (addition)
▲ Add three numbers by putting the largest number first and counting on or finding pairs which total 9, 10 or 11

Introducing the activity

▲ Practise adding three numbers, using a number line (0–20) to help model the additions. Locate the first number on the line and ask the children how many 'spaces' need to be jumped from the first number to the second number. Then jump the correct number of spaces again to match the third number. Emphasise 'spaces' not 'numbers'.

▲ Illustrate that the order of the addition does not matter, and that it is easiest to start with the larger number, and then jump on the two smaller numbers.

Main activity

▲ Before completing the sheet, discuss with the children that there may be different 'triples' on the elephant which have the same total.

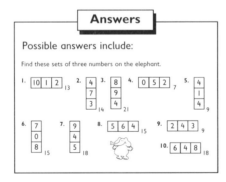

Answers

Possible answers include:

Find these sets of three numbers on the elephant.

1. 10 1 2 ₁₃
2. 4 7 3 ₁₄
3. 8 9 4 ₂₁
4. 0 5 2 ₇
5. 4 1 4 ₉
6. 7 0 8 ₁₅
7. 9 4 5 ₁₈
8. 5 6 4 ₁₅
9. 2 4 3 ₉
10. 6 4 8 ₁₈

Developments

▲ Investigate all the different possible triple totals on the elephant.
▲ Ask children to draw their own numbered elephant on squared paper, and then investigate the totals.
▲ Extend the elephant to contain numbers from 0 to 20, or 0 to 50.
▲ Shuffle a pack of playing cards (take out the picture cards), and make three piles. Reveal the top card on each pile and say the total of the numbers. Continue through the pack.

Materials

▲ Number line (0–20)
▲ Squared paper
▲ Number cards (1–10) or playing cards (without the picture cards)

Individual practice in Pupil Book 3
Activity 6 Adding three numbers

22

▲ cross-reference to the related Pupil Book activity

Each activity in the Teacher's Book comprises a page of teacher's notes and a photocopiable pupil page for group/pair work. The Pupil Book activities provide individual practice linked to the lessons in the Teacher's Book and offer an ideal resource for homework.

Teacher's Book 3

Elephant totals

6
Activity

This means: Find the part of the elephant which is this shape and has **three numbers with a total of eight**.

8

Here is one.

| 2 |
| 5 |
| 1 |
8

12

This means: Find the part of the elephant which is this shape and has **three numbers with a total of twelve**.

Here is one.

| 1 | 5 | 6 |
12

7	6	8	6			6	4
9	0	5	2	3	7	5	2	7
2	8		7	10	1	2	4	3
5			3	8	9	3	1	2
1			9	1	5	6	4	8
	4							9
3	5

Find these sets of three numbers on the ele

1. ⬜⬜⬜ 13

2. ⬜

3. ⬜ 14

4. ⬜ 21

6. ⬜ 15

7. ⬜ 18

8. ⬜⬜⬜

Individual practice/homework

▲ at least one page linked to the Teacher's Book activity of the same number
▲ answers are included in the Teacher's Book

Pupil page

▲ photocopiable game or activity to support group/pair work

Pupil Book 3

Adding three numbers

6
Activity

Copy and complete these additions.

| Example 1. 4 + 2 + 1 = 7 |

1. 4 + 2 + 1
2. 5 + 4 + 3
3. 6 + 3 + 2
4. 7 + 3 + 4
5. 5 + 6 + 2
6. 3 + 7 + 5
7. 9 + 1 + 4
8. 5 + 3 + 7

Write the total of the numbers on each strip.

| Example 9. 3 + 1 + 2 = 6 |

9. | 3 | 1 | 2 |

10. | 4 |
| 3 |
| 5 |

11. | 2 | 6 | 1 |

12. | 4 | 5 | 2 |

13. | 3 | 3 | 3 |

14. | 4 | 6 | 3 |

15. | 3 |
| 6 |
| 4 |

16. | 7 | 3 | 5 |

17. | 2 | 8 | 7 |

9

11

Numbering

Activity

Key vocabulary
digit
2-, 3-digit number
order
largest/ smallest
odd/even

Objectives

Place value and ordering
▲ Know the value of each digit in a 3-digit number
▲ Order a set of whole numbers
▲ Use the vocabulary of comparing and ordering 2-digit numbers
▲ Say the number that is 1, 10 or 100 more or less than a 3-digit number

Counting and properties of numbers
▲ Recognise 2-digit and 3-digit multiples of 2 and 5

Reasoning about numbers
▲ Solve a number problem, working systematically
▲ Investigate general statements about numbers

Introducing the activity

▲ Clarify the term 'digit', and the recognition of 2-digit, 3-digit... numbers.
▲ Read and say 3-digit numbers clearly, extending to 4-digit numbers.
  For example, write 762 on the board. The children read the number aloud as 'seven hundred and sixty-two'. Say a number, e.g. 'eight hundred and thirty-five'. Ask the children to write the number in digits as 835.
▲ Create different 2-digit numbers using three cards. How many are there altogether? (6)
▲ Choose a 3-digit number. Ask the children to give you the number which is 1, 10 and 100 more and less than the number.

Answers

The results are:

2-digit numbers	3-digit numbers
23 32 52 82	235 325 523 823
25 35 53 83	238 328 528 825
28 38 58 85	253 352 532 832
	258 358 538 835
	283 382 582 852
	285 385 583 853

4-digit numbers

2358	3258	5238	8235
2385	3285	5283	8253
2538	3528	5328	8352
2583	3582	5382	8325
2835	3825	5823	8523
2853	3852	5832	8532

Main activity

▲ Encourage children to work systematically, e.g. when finding 2-digit numbers, start with '1' in the tens place.

Developments

▲ Write the numbers in order from smallest to largest.
▲ Will there always be 12 different 2-digit numbers for any choice of four cards? Investigate.
▲ Investigate how many 4-digit numbers can be made.
▲ Investigate how many of the numbers are even and how many are odd for different choices of four digits. Can you see a pattern?

Materials
▲ Number cards (1–9)

Individual practice in Pupil Book 3
Activity 1 3-digit numbers

Numbering

You will need: these number cards

Make these different 2-digit numbers with the cards.

| 5 | 3 | | 2 | 8 | | 8 | 5 |

How many 2-digit numbers can you make altogether?

Now make these different 3-digit numbers.

| 3 | 5 | 2 | | 8 | 2 | 3 | | 5 | 3 | 8 |

How many 3-digit numbers can you make altogether?

Activity

Number box game

Key vocabulary

add
subtract

Objectives

Understanding addition and subtraction

▲ Continue to recognise that addition can be done in any order and add three or four single-digit numbers mentally

Rapid recall of addition/subtraction facts

▲ Know by heart addition and subtraction facts for numbers to 20

Reasoning about numbers

▲ Solve number puzzles, and recognise relationships about the positioning of the numbers in each equation

Introducing the activity

▲ Practise recalling addition facts and subtraction facts for numbers to 20.
▲ Enlarge the sheet, and write one number in a box for each calculation on the sheet. Ask the children to provide the other number(s) which will make the calculation correct.

Main activity

▲ Children play the game in pairs, or threes, each with a sheet of their own. Explain the rules:
  • The cards are shuffled and placed in a pile, face down.
  • Players take turns to reveal the top card. *All* players *either* write the revealed number in one of the boxes on their sheet, *or* they can choose to 'pass' and ignore it.
  • Once a number is written in a box, it can't be changed.
  • The winner is the first player to correctly complete all the calculations on their sheet.

Developments

▲ Investigate how many different possible solutions there are to each addition and subtraction in the game. For example, in the first addition, possible additions include: $4 + 9$, $5 + 8$, $6 + 7$.
▲ Invent a similar game, but change the calculations on the sheet.
▲ Stop when 15 cards have been revealed from the pile. The winner is the player who successfully completes the most calculations.
▲ Extend the calculations to include operations on 2-digit numbers.

Materials

▲ Three sets of number cards (0–9)

Individual practice in Pupil Book 3
Activity 2 Missing numbers

Number box game

2 Activity

You will need:

three sets of number cards (0–9)

1. ☐ + ☐ = **13**

2. ☐ − ☐ = **4**

3. ☐ + ☐ = **7**

4. ☐ − ☐ = **7**

5. ☐ + ☐ = **10**

6. ☐ − ☐ = **3**

7. ☐ + ☐ − ☐ = **5**

Six choices game

Key vocabulary

digit
3-digit number
largest/ smallest
odd/even
nearest/ furthest

Objectives

Counting and properties of numbers
▲ Recognise odd and even numbers

Place value and ordering
▲ Know the value of each digit in a 3-digit number
▲ Understand and use the vocabulary of comparing and ordering 3-digit numbers
▲ Compare two or more 3-digit numbers, and say which is the largest or smallest

Reasoning about numbers
▲ Explain methods and reasoning about numbers

Introducing the activity

▲ Using number cards (0–9), choose three cards and create different 3-digit numbers. Discuss which is the largest possible number, smallest, largest odd, smallest even, etc.

Main activity

▲ Children play the game in groups of 2–4, each with a sheet of their own. Explain the rules:
  • At the start of each round, the players decide on the target for that round and write it on the sheet. For example, the target for round 1 might be 'largest number', for round 2 it might be 'smallest number'. Other possibilities include: largest odd number, largest even number, smallest odd number, smallest even number.
  • One player throws the dice three times. After each throw, all players write the resulting number in one of their three 'dice number' boxes, finally creating a 3-digit number. Once a number is written in a box, it cannot be changed. Encourage the children to explain their reasoning in placing the numbers.
  • The players score as follows: if, for example, the target is 'largest number', then the player who has the largest scores 2 points, and the player with the next largest scores 1 point.
  • The overall winner is the player with most points after eight rounds.

Developments

▲ Play the game choosing different targets, e.g. nearest to 350, nearest to 410, furthest from 250, furthest from 330, largest odd number, smallest even number.

Materials

▲ Number cards (0–9)
▲ A dice

Individual practice in Pupil Book 3
Activity 3 Odds and evens

Six choices game

△ 3 **Activity**

You will need: one dice

target	dice number			score
1				
2				
3				
4				
5				
6				
7				
8				
			total	

Dicey times

Activity

Key vocabulary

multiply
score
product
largest/
smallest

Objectives

Understanding multiplication and division
▲ Understand multiplication and use the related vocabulary

Rapid recall of multiplication and division facts
▲ Begin to know multiplication facts up to 6 × 6

Reasoning about numbers
▲ Solve a number problem, working systematically, and recognise simple number patterns
▲ Investigate general statements about numbers

Introducing the activity

▲ Using squared paper, illustrate the concept of multiplication through square grids. Throw both dice, and, using the scores they show, draw a grid, i.e. for throws of 3 and 4, draw a 3 × 4 rectangular grid. Count how many squares are inside the grid. Read this as 'three fours are twelve'. Repeat for different throws of the dice. Challenge children to recall the multiplication fact without using squared paper.

Answers

The answers can be shown in a table.
The circled numbers are repeats.

1 × 1 = 1	2 × 1 = ②	3 × 1 = ③
1 × 2 = ②	2 × 2 = ④	3 × 2 = ⑥
1 × 3 = ③	2 × 3 = ⑥	3 × 3 = 9
1 × 4 = ④	2 × 4 = ⑧	3 × 4 = ⑫
1 × 5 = ⑤	2 × 5 = ⑩	3 × 5 = ⑮
1 × 6 = ⑥	2 × 6 = ⑫	3 × 6 = ⑱

4 × 1 = ④	5 × 1 = ⑤	6 × 1 = ⑥
4 × 2 = ⑧	5 × 2 = ⑩	6 × 2 = ⑫
4 × 3 = ⑫	5 × 3 = ⑮	6 × 3 = ⑱
4 × 4 = 16	5 × 4 = ⑳	6 × 4 = ㉔
4 × 5 = ⑳	5 × 5 = 25	6 × 5 = ㉚
4 × 6 = ㉔	5 × 6 = ㉚	6 × 6 = 36

There are 18 different possible answers.
1, 2, 3, 4, 5, 6, 8, 9, 10, 12, 15, 16, 18, 20, 24, 25, 30, 36

Main activity

▲ Start by throwing the two dice, randomly, and recording the different multiplications as they arise, using squared paper, as above, if necessary. (It is helpful to have two differently coloured dice, to encourage them to be seen as individual dice.)
▲ Encourage the children to move towards a systematic approach, e.g. suppose the red dice shows a '1' – ask them to predict what scores are possible for different throws of the green dice.

Developments

▲ Discuss the largest and smallest possible product.
▲ Ask: If the answer is 12, what scores are possible on each dice?
▲ Extend to numbering the dice differently, e.g. write 1, 2, 3, 4, 5, 10 on the faces of two blank cubes.

Materials

▲ Squared paper
▲ Two dice
▲ Two blank cubes

Individual practice in Pupil Book 3
Activity 4 Multiplying
Activity 4b More multiplying

Dicey times

You will need: two dice

These dice have been thrown, and their scores multiplied together.

$6 \times 6 = 36$

$2 \times 6 = 12$

$4 \times 1 = 4$

Investigate how many different possible answers there are.

5

Activity

Drinks

Objectives

Organising and using data

▲ Organise and interpret data in simple tables

Introducing the activity

▲ Using the sheet, help children to interpret the table by asking a series of questions, such as:
  • Which drinks does Hamish like? dislike?
  • How many of the five drinks does Katie like? dislike?
  • Who likes all five drinks?
  • Which drink does everyone like?
  • How many of the five children like milk? orange juice...?
  • Which children like tea? water...?
  • How many children don't like water? tea...?
  • Which drink is the most popular? least popular?
  • Who likes the least number of drinks? Who likes the most?

Main activity

▲ Sort the children into groups to construct their own table based on taste in drinks. Each group records their likes and dislikes for the same five drinks shown on the sheet.

▲ The groups can then construct a new table based on their own choice of five drinks. Encourage them to ask and answer questions of their own based on the table.

Developments

▲ Extend the activity to constructing a table based on taste in something other than drinks, e.g. foods, television programmes, comics.

Materials

▲ Squared paper (large squares)

Individual practice in Pupil Book 3
Activity 5 Reading a table

Drinks

Drinks we like

	milk	lemonade	water	tea	orange juice
Hamish	✗	✓	✓	✗	✗
Mina	✓	✓	✓	✓	✓
Katie	✗	✓	✗	✗	✓
Amil	✓	✓	✓	✗	✓
Emily	✗	✓	✓	✗	✓

Elephant totals

Objectives

Understanding addition and subtraction
▲ Extend understanding of addition and recognise that it can be done in any order
▲ Add three single-digit numbers mentally

Rapid recall of addition facts
▲ Recall addition facts for numbers to 20

Mental calculation strategies (addition)
▲ Add three numbers by putting the largest number first and counting on or finding pairs which total 9, 10 or 11

Introducing the activity

▲ Practise adding three numbers, using a number line (0–20) to help model the additions. Locate the first number on the line and ask the children how many 'spaces' need to be jumped from the first number to the second number. Then jump the correct number of spaces again to match the third number. Emphasise 'spaces' not 'numbers'.

▲ Illustrate that the order of the addition does not matter, and that it is easiest to start with the larger number, and then jump on the two smaller numbers.

Main activity

▲ Before completing the sheet, discuss with the children that there may be different 'triples' on the elephant which have the same total.

Answers

Possible answers include:

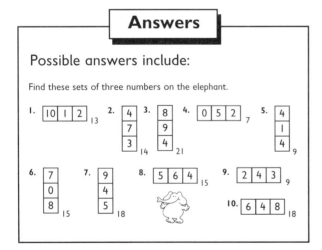

Developments

▲ Investigate all the different possible triple totals on the elephant.
▲ Ask children to draw their own numbered elephant on squared paper, and then investigate the totals.
▲ Extend the elephant to contain numbers from 0 to 20, or 0 to 50.
▲ Shuffle a pack of playing cards (take out the picture cards), and make three piles. Reveal the top card on each pile and say the total of the numbers. Continue through the pack.

Materials

▲ Number line (0–20)
▲ Squared paper
▲ Number cards (1–10) or playing cards (without the picture cards)

> **Individual practice in Pupil Book 3**
> Activity 6 Adding three numbers

Elephant totals

Activity 6

This means: Find the part of the elephant which is this shape and has **three numbers with a total of eight**.

8

Here is one.

2
5
1

8

12

This means: Find the part of the elephant which is this shape and has **three numbers with a total of twelve**.

Here is one.

1	5	6

12

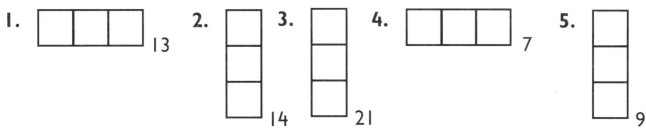

Find these sets of three numbers on the elephant.

1. 13

2. 14

3. 21

4. 7

5. 9

6. 15

7. 18

8. 15

9. 9

10. 18

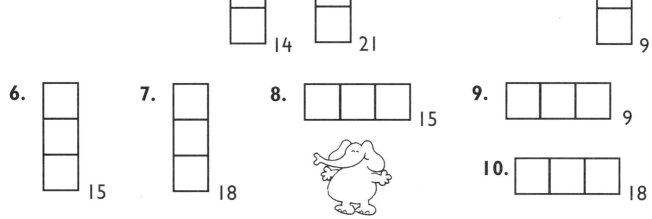

Number trails

Key vocabulary

up/down
across
diagonal
total
smallest/
largest

Objectives

Understanding addition and subtraction
▲ Understand addition and recognise that it can be done in any order
▲ Add three or four single-digit numbers mentally

Rapid recall of addition facts
▲ Know all addition facts for numbers to 20

Mental calculation strategies (addition)
▲ Add several small numbers by finding pairs which total 10

Introducing the activity

▲ Practise adding several numbers, using a number line (1–20) to help model the additions. Locate the first number on the line. Jump the correct number of 'spaces' along the line to match the second number, then the third, and so on.
▲ Illustrate that the order of the addition does not matter, and that it is easiest to pair some numbers together, e.g. (2 + 1) + (3 + 5) + 4 can be changed to 3 + 8 + 4. Encourage children to look for pairs or sets which total 10.

Answers

If the first move is upward, then possible trails are:

  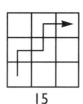

totals: 18   18   15

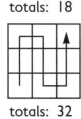 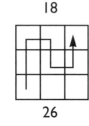 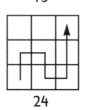

totals: 32   26   24

If the first move is across, then possible trails are:

totals: 17   12   15

   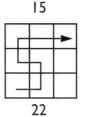

totals: 32   22   22

Main activity

▲ Assume that diagonal moves are not allowed, only horizontal and vertical moves can be made.

Developments

▲ Investigate all the different possible trails.
▲ Discuss which trail gives the smallest/ largest total.
▲ Extend to a grid with numbers 1–9.
▲ Change the shape of the grid.

Materials

▲ Number line (1–20)
▲ Squared paper

Individual practice in Pupil Book 3
Activity 7 Adding

Number trails

Activity 7

You will need:
squared paper

Draw this number square.

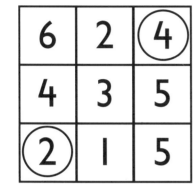

6	2	④	finish
4	3	5	
②	1	5	

start

Now draw this trail from **start** to **finish**.

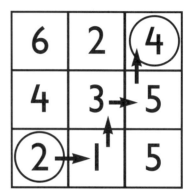

6	2	④	finish
4	3→5		
②→1		5	

start

This trail is: 2 + 1 + 3 + 5 + 4 = 15

Find some different trails from **start** to **finish**. Record them here.

8

Activity

Difference game

Key vocabulary

difference
smaller/
larger
total

Objectives

Understanding addition and subtraction

▲ Understand addition and subtraction and use the related vocabulary

Rapid recall of addition/subtraction facts

▲ Know addition and subtraction facts for numbers to 20

Mental calculation strategies (subtraction)

▲ Find a small difference by counting up from the smaller to the larger number

▲ Use known number facts and place value to add/subtract mentally

Introducing the activity

▲ Practise finding differences, using a number line (1–30) as a model. Choose two numbers, locate their position on the line, and find the difference by counting on from the smaller to the larger.

▲ Give the children a number, and ask them to find two numbers whose difference matches it.

Main activity

▲ Children play the game in pairs. Explain the rules:

  • Each player chooses a board, left or right. They take turns to throw both dice, and find the total, e.g. for throws of 3 and 5, the total is 8.

  • Next, each player finds two numbers on their board which have a difference that matches this total, i.e. the difference is 8. So, for example, one player might choose 18 and 10, and place a counter on each number. If one or both players can't cover two numbers, then they do nothing.

  • The winner is the first to cover their board with counters.

Developments

▲ Investigate different possible pairs of numbers whose difference matches a dice total.

▲ Change the numbering of the dice, e.g. write 5–10 on the faces of a blank cube, and use it together with a 1–6 dice.

▲ Throw three dice instead of two.

▲ When one player has covered their board, the loser scores points to match the total of all uncovered numbers. Players aim for the lowest score over a set number of games.

Materials

▲ Number line (1–30)

▲ Three dice

▲ A set of counters for each player

▲ A blank dice

Individual practice in Pupil Book 3
Activity 8 Differences

Difference game

You will need: two dice

a set of counters each

Player B

1	2	3	4
5	6	7	8
9	10	11	12
13	14	15	16
17	18	19	20
21	22	23	24

Player A

1	2	3	4
5	6	7	8
9	10	11	12
13	14	15	16
17	18	19	20
21	22	23	24

Word lengths

Key vocabulary

data
tally chart
total
bar chart
most/least
common
frequency
more/
less than

Objectives

Estimating and rounding

▲ Use the vocabulary of estimation and begin to make sensible estimates

Organising and using data

▲ Collect data and record it in a tally chart/frequency table
▲ Construct and interpret a bar chart

Introducing the activity

▲ Discuss the meaning of word length. Invite children to suggest words which have a word length of three letters, four letters…
▲ Look at the text on the sheet and read it together. Ask children to find a word which has two letters, three letters…
▲ Ask children to predict which word length occurs most often/least often in this passage.
▲ Ask children to estimate how many 3-letter words, 4-letter words… there are.

Main activity

▲ The children count the number of letters in each word, and record each with a tally mark in the chart on the sheet.
▲ The data can then be represented by means of a bar chart.
▲ Follow this by asking questions to help children interpret the chart, such as:
  • How many words have five letters? three letters…?
  • Which word length occurred, say, five times?
  • Which word length was the least/most common?
▲ Compare the children's estimates with the actual data.

Developments

▲ The children choose one of their own pieces of writing and construct a tally chart followed by a bar chart to illustrate the data.
▲ Choose a piece of text from each of two books/newspapers. Select a section of exactly 50 or 100 words for each. Analyse and compare the data for the two.
▲ Extend to analysing the frequency of use of each letter in the text.
▲ Extend to analysing sentence length.

Materials

▲ Squared paper
▲ Books/newspapers

Answers

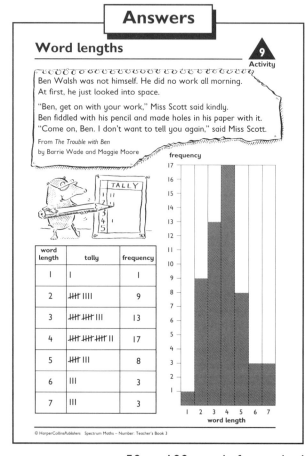

Word lengths

Ben Walsh was not himself. He did no work all morning. At first, he just looked into space.

"Ben, get on with your work," Miss Scott said kindly.
Ben fiddled with his pencil and made holes in his paper with it.
"Come on, Ben. I don't want to tell you again," said Miss Scott.

From *The Trouble with Ben*
by Barrie Wade and Maggie Moore

word length	tally	frequency
1	I	1
2	JHT IIII	9
3	JHT JHT III	13
4	JHT JHT JHT II	17
5	JHT III	8
6	III	3
7	III	3

© HarperCollinsPublishers Spectrum Maths – Number: Teacher's Book 3

Individual practice in Pupil Book 3
Activity 9 Bar chart

Word lengths

Ben Walsh was not himself. He did no work all morning.
At first, he just looked into space.

"Ben, get on with your work," Miss Scott said kindly.
Ben fiddled with his pencil and made holes in his paper with it.
"Come on, Ben. I don't want to tell you again," said Miss Scott.

From *The Trouble with Ben*
by Barrie Wade and Maggie Moore

frequency

word length	tally	frequency
1		
2		
3		
4		
5		
6		
7		

17
16
15
14
13
12
11
10
9
8
7
6
5
4
3
2
1

1   2   3   4   5   6   7
word length

Fraction wheels game

10 Activity

Key vocabulary

fraction
equal parts
one half
one third
two thirds
one… four quarters

Objectives

Fractions

- ▲ Recognise and name $\frac{1}{2}$, $\frac{1}{3}$, $\frac{1}{6}$ and use them to find fractions of shapes
- ▲ Begin to recognise fractions of several parts of a whole, e.g. $\frac{2}{3}$
- ▲ Begin to recognise the concept of equivalent fractions, e.g. $\frac{1}{2}$ and $\frac{3}{6}$

Introducing the activity

- ▲ Draw large circles divided into sixths, as on the sheet.
- ▲ Discuss the different fractions by colouring sectors of the circle, asking children to name the fraction.
- ▲ Invite children to colour different fractions of the circle.
- ▲ Extend this to circles divided into different numbers of equal parts, e.g. 4.

Main activity

- ▲ Children play the game in pairs, each with a copy of the sheet. Explain the rules:
  - Starting with the top board, players take turns to throw the dice, and colour a part of any wheel which matches the dice throw.
  - Players do not have to complete one wheel before colouring another.
  - On one turn, players can only colour one wheel.
  - The winner is the first to completely colour all eight wheels.
  - The second board can be used to play again.

Developments

- ▲ Make two identical dice, both numbered $\frac{1}{6}$, $\frac{1}{3}$, $\frac{1}{2}$, $\frac{2}{6}$, $\frac{2}{6}$, $\frac{2}{3}$. Throw both dice, and choose which fraction to colour on the sheet.
- ▲ Make a new set of boards, by dividing the circles into eighths, and use a dice labelled $\frac{1}{8}$, $\frac{1}{4}$, $\frac{1}{2}$, $\frac{3}{8}$, $\frac{3}{4}$, $\frac{5}{8}$.

Materials

- ▲ Blank cubes
- ▲ Card to make new boards

Individual practice in Pupil Book 3
Activity 10 Fractions

Fraction wheels game

You will need: a dice made by writing $\frac{1}{6}$, $\frac{1}{3}$, $\frac{1}{2}$, $\frac{2}{6}$, $\frac{3}{6}$, $\frac{2}{3}$ on the faces of a cube

Activity

11

Key vocabulary

double

treble

Singles, doubles and trebles

Objectives

Understanding addition and subtraction

▲ Add three or four 2-digit numbers with pencil and paper

Mental calculation strategies (+ and −)

▲ Partition into 5 and a bit when adding 6, 7, 8 or add 9 by adding 10 and adjusting by 1

Rapid recall of multiplication facts

▲ Know multiplication facts for the 2 and 3 times-tables and begin to know the 3 and 4 times-tables
▲ Derive quickly doubles of numbers to 20 and doubles of multiples of 5 to 100

Introducing the activity

▲ Practise doubling numbers up to 10. Confirm that double 4 is 4 + 4, for example. Use towers of interlocking cubes to serve as a model to illustrate the total. Extend to practising trebling, e.g. treble 10 is 10 + 10 + 10.
▲ Give hints to help the adding when writing the running total. For example:
  • look for units digits which make 10, e.g. 16 + 4 = 20
  • split a number into parts to make digits which add to 10, e.g. 16 + 7 = 16 + 4 + 3 = 23
  • add 9 by adding 10, then subtracting 1, e.g. 16 + 9 = 26 − 1 = 25.

Main activity

▲ Children play the game in pairs, each with a score sheet. Explain the rules:
  • Shuffle the number cards (0–10) and place them in a pile, face down.
  • Players take turns to reveal the top card, then throw the dice to see if the card number is to be singled (S), doubled (D) or trebled (T), e.g. 7 followed by D, gives a score of 14.
  • Players enter their score on the score sheet.
  • Continue, with each player writing down their own scores, and keeping a running total in the last column, until the winner reaches a total of 80.

Developments

▲ Change the rules so that the winner is the *last* player to reach 80 points.
▲ Extend the range of numbers on the cards, e.g. 1–15, 1–20, multiples of 10, multiples of 5 to 50.
▲ Each player starts with a score of 100, and the score in each round is subtracted from the total. The winner is the first to reach zero points.

Materials

▲ A blank cube
▲ Two sets of number cards (0–10)

| **Individual practice in Pupil Book 3** |
| Activity 11 Doubling |

Singles, doubles and trebles

You will need: two sets of number cards (0–10)
a cube with S, S, D, D, T, T
written on the faces

number	S, D or T	score	total

number	S, D or T	score	total

number	S, D or T	score	total

number	S, D or T	score	total

Activity 12

Paired see-saw numbers

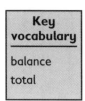

Key vocabulary

balance

total

Objectives

Understanding addition and subtraction
▲ Extend understanding of addition and recognise that it can be done in any order

Rapid recall of addition/subtraction facts
▲ Know by heart addition facts for all numbers to 15

Reasoning about numbers
▲ Solve a simple number problem, working systematically

Introducing the activity

▲ Draw a large see-saw with a given 'base number'. Discuss the different pairs of numbers which can be placed on each side of the see-saw. Blu-tak number cards in position on each side to make it balance. Repeat for different possible choices of pairs of cards.

▲ Discuss whether 3 above 5 on the see-saw is the same as 5 above 3, for example. It is simpler to assume that they are the same.

▲ Explain that there are often several different possible solutions to each see-saw.

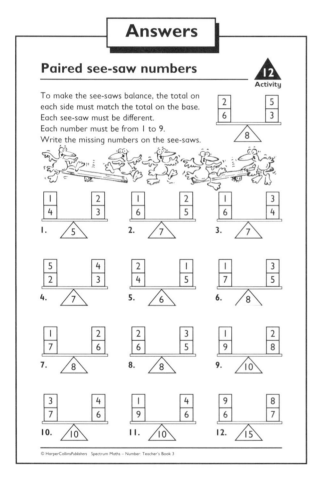

Main activity

▲ Prepare a large outline of a see-saw for the children to use with the number cards. They should then record their answers on the sheet.

Developments

▲ Investigate how many different ways there are of balancing the see-saw with a base number of 10. Extend to other totals.

▲ Extend to different see-saws, e.g. three numbers on one side and two on the other.

▲ Extend to allowing numbers greater than 9.

Materials

▲ Number cards (1–9)
▲ Blu-tak
▲ A large see-saw outline

> **Individual practice in Pupil Book 3**
> Activity 12 Balancing totals

Paired see-saw numbers

To make the see-saws balance, the total on
each side must match the total on the base.
Each see-saw must be different.
Each number must be from 1 to 9.
Write the missing numbers on the see-saws.

| | |
|2| |5|
|6| |3|

8

1. /5\

2. /7\

3. /7\

4. /7\

5. /6\

6. /8\

7. /8\

8. /8\

9. /10\

10. /10\

11. /10\

12. /15\

Difference race

Objectives

Place value and ordering
▲ Use the vocabulary of comparing ordinal numbers, e.g. first, second, etc.

Rapid recall of addition/subtraction facts
▲ Know by heart subtraction facts for numbers to 6

Reasoning about numbers
▲ Solve a simple number problem, leading to generalisation and prediction
▲ Explain methods and reasoning about numbers

Introducing the activity

▲ Clarify the meaning of 'difference' by throwing two dice and making two towers of cubes to match the two dice numbers. Put the towers side by side. Ask the children to suggest how many more cubes need to be added to the smaller to reach the larger.

Main activity

▲ Children play the game in pairs. Explain the rules:
  • Each player chooses three horses in the race, placing counters over the numbers at the 'start', e.g:

  Encourage the children to predict and explain their methods in choosing their lanes.
  • The two dice are thrown and the players work out the difference between the two dice numbers.
  • The horse whose start number matches this difference advances one space forwards.
  • The winner is the player who owns the horse which reaches 'finish' first.

Developments

▲ Continue the game to see which horse comes second, which third.
▲ Keep a record of the number of times each horse wins.
▲ Investigate different ways of arriving at a difference of 0, a difference of 1, a difference of 2... Do some horses have better chances than others?
▲ Create a variation of the game. Make a dice numbered 1–6, and another numbered 5–10, by writing on blank cubes. Decide on all the possible differences (0–9), and draw a race track to match this (i.e. with 10 tracks). Play the game several times.

Materials

▲ Two dice
▲ Three counters in each of two colours
▲ Blank cubes

Individual practice in Pupil Book 3
Activity 13 More differences

Difference race

Activity 13

You will need: two dice

three counters each

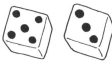 

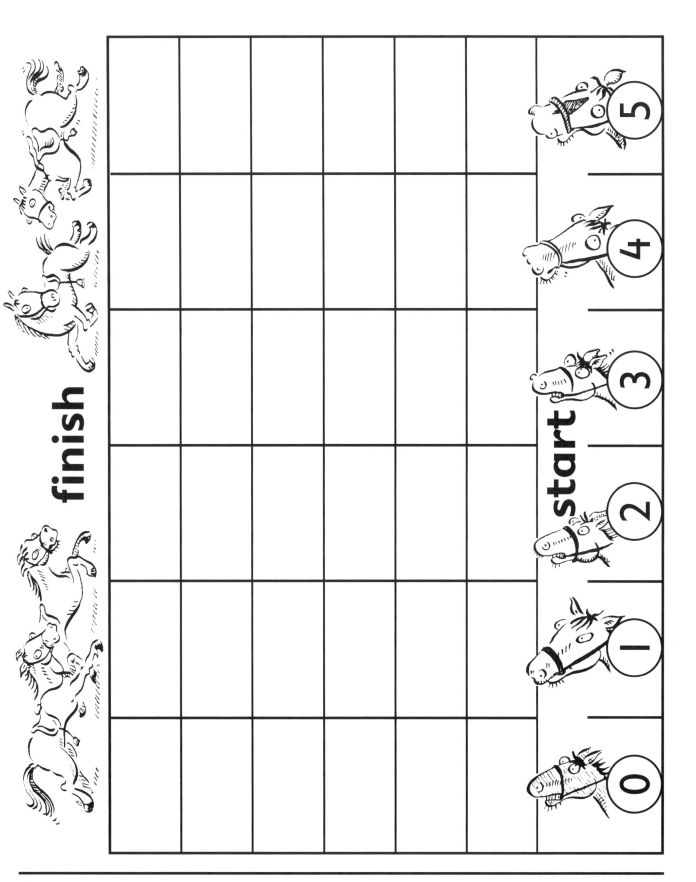

Difference pairs

Activity

Key vocabulary

difference
pair
smaller/
larger
total

Objectives

Understanding addition and subtraction
▲ Extend understanding of subtraction and use the related vocabulary

Rapid recall of subtraction facts
▲ Know by heart subtraction facts for all numbers to 20

Reasoning about numbers
▲ Recognise simple number patterns

Introducing the activity

▲ Clarify the meaning of 'difference' using a number line (1–20). Choose two number cards, locate each of them on the line, and count on from the smaller to reach the larger, finding the difference between them.

Answers

There are nine pairs with a difference of 9.

| 1 | 10 | 2 | 11 | 3 | 12 | 4 | 13 | 5 | 14 |

| 6 | 15 | 7 | 16 | 8 | 17 | 9 | 18 |

The results for other differences can be tabulated.

7	8	9	10
1, 8	1, 9	1, 10	1, 11
2, 9	2, 10	2, 11	2, 12
3, 10	3, 11	3, 12	3, 13
4, 11	4, 12	4, 13	4, 14
5, 12	5, 13	5, 14	5, 15
6, 13	6, 14	6, 15	6, 16
7, 14	7, 15	7, 16	7, 17
	8, 16	8, 17	8, 18
		9, 18	9, 19
			10, 20

11	12	13
1, 12	1, 13	1, 14
2, 13	2, 14	2, 15
3, 14	3, 15	3, 16
4, 15	4, 16	4, 17
5, 16	5, 17	5, 18
6, 17	6, 18	6, 19
7, 18	7, 19	7, 20
8, 19	8, 20	
9, 20		

Explain that some cards can be paired with more than one other number card to create the same difference, i.e.
$8 - 1 = 7$ and
$15 - 8 = 7$.

Main activity

▲ Encourage the children to work systematically, looking for a pattern. For example, to find pairs with a difference of 9, start with 1 and find its partner, then find the partner to card 2, and so on.

Developments

▲ Ask the children: For which differences can all cards be paired off?
▲ Extend to using a different set of cards, e.g. 5–20.
▲ Investigate pairs which have the same total, instead of difference.

Materials

▲ Number line (1–20)
▲ Number cards (1–20)

Individual practice in Pupil Book 3
Activity 14 Coin differences

Difference pairs

You will need: number cards (1–20)

All these pairs
have a difference of $\boxed{7}$

| 1 | 2 | 3 | 4 | 5 | 6 | 7 | 8 | 9 | 10 |

| 11 | 12 | 13 | 14 | 15 | 16 | 17 | 18 | 19 | 20 |

$\boxed{1}$ $\boxed{8}$ $\boxed{4}$ $\boxed{11}$ $\boxed{3}$ $\boxed{10}$ $\boxed{5}$ $\boxed{12}$

$\boxed{2}$ $\boxed{9}$ $\boxed{7}$ $\boxed{14}$ $\boxed{6}$ $\boxed{13}$

How many pairs can you make with a difference of 9?
Record your work here.

Investigate for other differences.

Addition pyramids

Objectives

Understanding addition and subtraction
▲ Extend understanding that subtraction is the inverse of addition

Rapid recall of addition/subtraction facts
▲ Know addition and subtraction facts for all numbers to 20

Mental calculation strategies (addition and subtraction)
▲ Put the largest number first and/or find pairs totalling 10
▲ Add 9 by adding 10 and subtracting 1
▲ Say a subtraction fact corresponding to an addition fact

Reasoning about numbers
▲ Solve simple number puzzles, working systematically

Introducing the activity

▲ Practise recall of addition facts using number cards (1–9). Blu-tak three in a row (as if they are the bottom layer of the pyramid). Discuss the total of the first two, and write this above them. Do the same for the second and third. Finally, find the total of the two numbers in the second row, to complete the pyramid. Repeat this for different sets of three or four cards.

Key vocabulary

total
layer
first,
second,
third

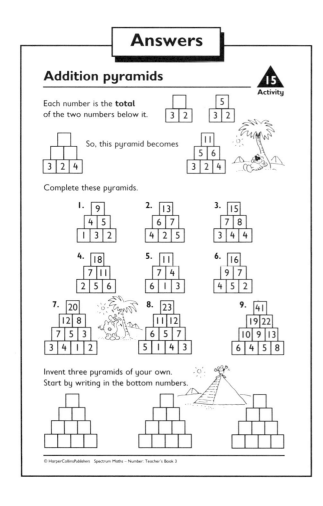

Main activity

▲ The first row of pyramids require adding pairs from the bottom. Some in the other rows require subtraction. Suggest helpful strategies such as those listed in objectives above.

Developments

▲ Investigate the top brick number for a bottom layer of 1, 2, 3, 4. Investigate different arrangements of 1, 2, 3 and 4 in the bottom layer, and how, if at all, this affects the top brick number.
▲ Construct an addition pyramid which has a given top number, e.g. 20. Start at the top, writing 20 on the top brick, then write two numbers below it which have a total of 20, e.g. 14 and 6, and so on.
▲ Construct addition pyramids of different sizes.

Materials

▲ Number cards (1–9)
▲ Blu-tak
▲ Pyramid paper (see photocopiable sheet on p. 93)

Individual practice in Pupil Book 3
Activity 15 More addition pyramids

Addition pyramids

Each number is the **total**
of the two numbers below it.

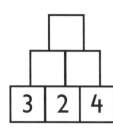

So, this pyramid becomes

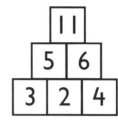

Complete these pyramids.

1.
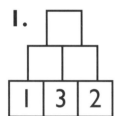

2.

3.

4.

5.
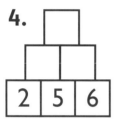

6.
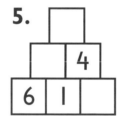

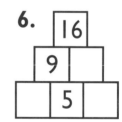

7.
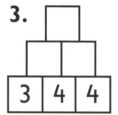

8.

9.

Invent three pyramids of your own.
Start by writing in the bottom numbers.

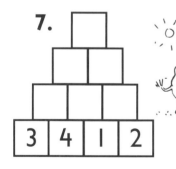

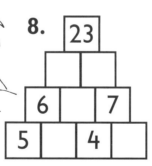

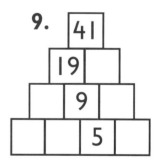

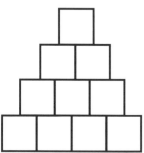

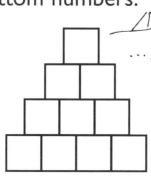

16 Activity

Fill the purses

Objectives

Counting and properties of numbers
▲ Recognise 2-digit multiples of 5 or 10

Understanding addition and subtraction
▲ Continue to recognise that addition can be done in any order and add three or four single-digit numbers mentally

Problems involving 'real life' or money
▲ Solve money problems, working out which coins to pay; explain how the problem was solved
▲ Recognise all coins and money notation

Introducing the activity

▲ Give the children two of each coin: 5p, 10p, 20p. Ask the children to show you:
  • 20p with 2 coins
  • 15p with 2 coins
  • 20p with 3 coins
  • 30p with 2 coins...
▲ Discuss the correct solution each time, using children to demonstrate.

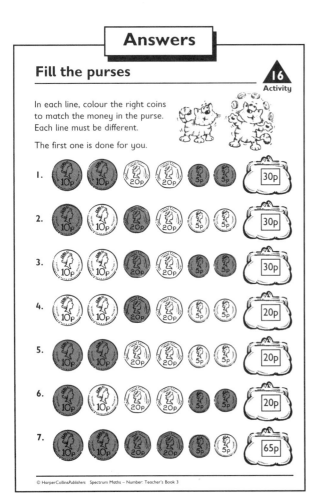

Main activity

▲ Encourage the children to use coins to help them find the solutions, before colouring the coins on the sheet. For example, use a collection of 5p, 10p and 20p coins. Explore different ways of making the target 20p, for example, by laying out different combinations of the coins.

Developments

▲ Investigate what other totals can be made by colouring these coins. It is possible to make these totals: 5p, 10p, 15p, 20p, 25p, 30p, 35p, 40p, 45p, 50p, 55p, 60p, 65p, 70p.
▲ Investigate which of the above amounts can be made in different ways.
▲ Conduct similar investigations to the above, but using a different set of coins, e.g. 1p, 2p, 5p, 10p or 10p, 20p, 50p, £1.

Materials

▲ Coins: 1p, 2p, 5p, 10p, 20p, 50p, £1

Fill the purses

In each line, colour the right coins
to match the money in the purse.
Each line must be different.

The first one is done for you.

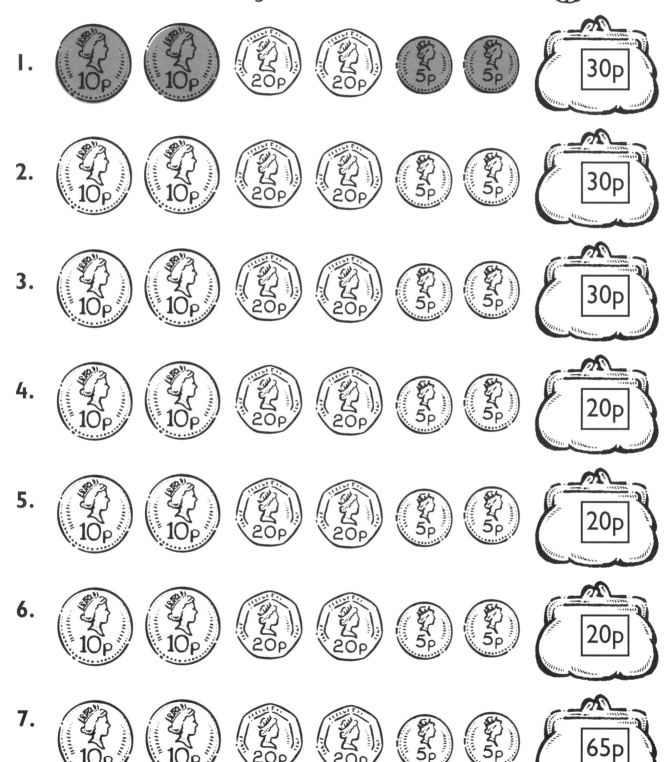

1. 10p 10p 20p 20p 5p 5p **30p**

2. 10p 10p 20p 20p 5p 5p **30p**

3. 10p 10p 20p 20p 5p 5p **30p**

4. 10p 10p 20p 20p 5p 5p **20p**

5. 10p 10p 20p 20p 5p 5p **20p**

6. 10p 10p 20p 20p 5p 5p **20p**

7. 10p 10p 20p 20p 5p 5p **65p**

Activity 17

Key vocabulary

consecutive

total

Consecutive trains

Objectives

Understanding addition and subtraction
▲ Add several single-digit numbers mentally

Mental calculation strategies (addition)
▲ Put the largest number first and/or find pairs totalling 9, 10 or 11

Reasoning about numbers
▲ Recognise simple patterns and relationships concerning consecutive numbers

Introducing the activity

▲ Introduce consecutive numbers by counting on in ones together from any starting number.
▲ Clarify the concept of 'consecutive' numbers using sets of number cards (1–9). Make pairs of consecutive numbers, and ask the children to suggest the totals. Extend to making sets of three consecutive numbers, then four and so on.
▲ Challenge the children to work in reverse, by asking, for example: Show me two consecutive cards whose total is 9. Show me three consecutive cards whose total is 9, etc.

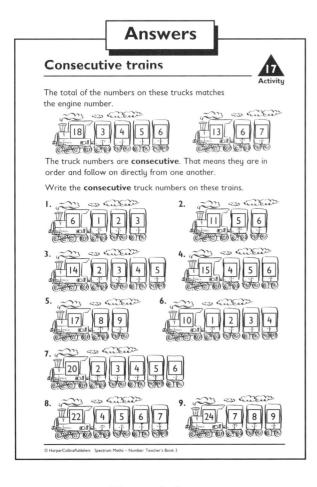

Main activity

▲ After completing the sheet, challenge the children to make consecutive trains for all engine numbers from 1 to 20. Investigate which are possible and which are not. Discuss the pattern in the impossible trains: 1, 2, 4, 8, 16.

Developments

▲ Investigate for which engine numbers different trains can be made. For example, engine number 15 can be made with two trucks: 7 and 8; with three trucks: 4, 5 and 6; and with five trucks: 1, 2, 3, 4 and 5.
▲ Extend the engine numbers beyond 20.
▲ Investigate all the engine numbers which can have two trucks, i.e. 3, 5, 7, 9, 11... the odd numbers except 1.
▲ Investigate all the engine numbers which can have three trucks, i.e. 6, 9, 12, 15, 18... the multiples of 3 except 3.

Materials

▲ Number cards (1–9)

Individual practice in Pupil Book 3
Activity 17 Next-door numbers

44

Consecutive trains

The total of the numbers on these trucks matches
the engine number.

The truck numbers are **consecutive**. That means they are in
order and follow on directly from one another.

Write the **consecutive** truck numbers on these trains.

1. 6

2. 11

3. 14

4. 15

5. 17

6. 10

7. 20

8. 22

9. 24

Five card game

Key vocabulary

hundreds, tens, ones

3-digit number

largest/ smallest

even/odd

nearest

closest

Objectives

Place value and ordering

▲ Recognise the value of each digit in a 3-digit number and partition numbers into hundreds, tens, ones (HTU)

▲ Compare and order 3-digit numbers and use the related vocabulary

Estimating and rounding

▲ Round 3-digit numbers to their nearest 10, 100

Reasoning about numbers

▲ Explain methods and reasoning about numbers

Introducing the activity

▲ Choose three cards from the number cards (1–9) and create different 3-digit numbers using the cards. Discuss which is the largest possible number, smallest, largest odd, smallest even etc.

▲ Extend the above to Include the concept of nearest number to 400, for example. Use a 100 division number line to illustrate.

Main activity

▲ Children play the game in groups of 2–4, each with a score sheet. Explain the rules:

• Each player shuffles their set of cards and deals themselves five. These are the only cards that they can use for the game.

• Starting with round 1, players choose any three of their five cards and try to match the target, placing the cards in position on their sheet. For example, if the player's five cards are 1, 3, 4, 5, 7, then in round 1 (largest number) he/she would choose cards 4, 5 and 7 and make 754, the largest number that can be made with these three cards.

• For each round, the player closest to the target number scores 3 points, the next closest scores 2 points and the next closest scores 1 point.

• At the end of the eight rounds, the winner is the player with the most points. The board allows the game to be played twice.

Developments

▲ Introduce the zero card.

▲ Instead of five cards, deal four or six.

▲ Extend the game to 4-digit numbers.

▲ Change the targets, e.g. nearest to any hundred, smallest multiple of 3…

Materials

▲ Number cards (1–9), a set for each player

▲ Number line (1–100)

Individual practice in Pupil Book 3
Activity 18 3-card numbers

Five card game

Activity 18

You will need: a set of number cards each (1−9)

hundreds	tens	units

round and target	game 1	points	game 2	points
1 largest number				
2 smallest number				
3 largest even number				
4 nearest to 400				
5 furthest away from 320				
6 smallest even number				
7 nearest to 650				
8 largest odd number				

Subtraction machines

Objectives

Understanding addition and subtraction
▲ Extend understanding of subtraction
▲ Consolidate subtraction as the inverse of addition

Rapid recall of addition/subtraction facts
▲ Know subtraction facts for all numbers to 20

Mental calculation strategies (subtraction)
▲ Find a small difference by counting up from the smaller to the larger number
▲ Say an addition fact corresponding to a subtraction fact and vice versa

Introducing the activity

▲ Discuss the concept of a subtraction machine using number cards (0–20). Choose a particular machine, e.g. 'take 2', and discuss the results when putting random numbers through the machine. Use a number line (1–20) to model the subtraction. Demonstrate how to complete the 'in/out' tables.
▲ Extend to different machines, e.g. 'take 10' for number cards 10–20.

Answers

1. take 4

in	out
9	5
7	3
6	2
10	6
5	1
12	8

2. take 2

in	out
5	3
8	6
3	1
10	8
7	5
13	11

3. take 8

in	out
9	1
14	6
8	0
18	10
10	2
12	4

4. take 1

in	out
3	2
9	8
14	13
7	6
21	20
4	3

5. take 5

in	out
11	6
17	12
24	19
9	4
37	32
12	7

6. take 7

in	out
8	1
10	3
13	6
9	2
15	8
20	13

7. take 3

in	out
8	5
10	7
13	10
9	6
15	12
20	17

8. take 6

in	out
8	2
10	4
13	7
9	3
15	9
20	14

Main activity

▲ Questions 2 and 3 require straightforward subtractions. In questions 4 and 5, the children need to recognise that, given numbers in the 'out' column, they need to decide which number went 'in'.

Developments

▲ Use larger numbers in the machines.
▲ Introduce two machines together, e.g. 'take 3' and 'take 5'. Numbers go through both machines one after the other. Ask the children: Does it matter which order?
▲ Explore different machines, e.g. adding machines.
▲ Construct tables for 'double' and 'half' machines.
▲ Construct multiplication machines, e.g. '× 3' machines.

Materials

▲ Number cards (0–20)
▲ Number line (1–20)

Individual practice in Pupil Book 3
Activity 19 Taking away

Subtraction machines

This is a **take 4** machine.
When 9 is put **in**, 5 comes **out**.
Complete this table for the **take 4** machine.

1.

in	out
9	5
7	
6	
10	
5	
12	

Complete the tables for these machines.

2.

in	out
5	
8	
3	
10	
7	
13	

3.

in	out
9	
14	
8	
18	
10	
12	

4.

in	out
3	
	8
	13
7	
	20
4	

5.

in	out
11	
	12
	19
9	
	32
12	

Draw tables to show what comes **out** when 8, 10, 13, 9, 15 and 20 are put **in** these machines.

6. 　　**7.** 　　**8.**

Names and vowels

Key
vocabulary

tally chart
bar chart
frequency

Objectives

Organising and using data
▲ Collect data and record it in a tally chart/frequency table
▲ Construct and interpret a bar chart

Estimating and rounding
▲ Use the vocabulary of estimation and approximation

Introducing the activity

▲ Discuss which letters are vowels, and list them.
▲ Look at the sheet, and ask questions to help the children interpret the data, such as:
  • Which names contain the letter 'o'?
  • Which name/s use two 'a's?
  • Can you find a name which uses an 'o' and an 'a'?
  • Which are the vowels in Nicola?
  • How many vowels are there in Elizabeth?
  • Which names use two vowels? three vowels?
  • Which name contains the most vowels?
  • Which names use two different vowels?
  • Which names use the same vowel twice?
  • Which names contain two non-vowels (consonants)?
▲ Estimate how many 'e's, vowels and non-vowels there are altogether.

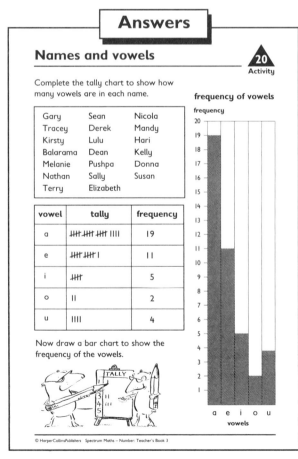

Answers

Names and vowels

△ 20
Activity

Complete the tally chart to show how many vowels are in each name.

Gary	Sean	Nicola
Tracey	Derek	Mandy
Kirsty	Lulu	Hari
Balarama	Dean	Kelly
Melanie	Pushpa	Donna
Nathan	Sally	Susan
Terry	Elizabeth	

vowel	tally	frequency
a	JHT JHT JHT IIII	19
e	JHT JHT I	11
i	JHT	5
o	II	2
u	IIII	4

Now draw a bar chart to show the frequency of the vowels.

frequency of vowels

© HarperCollinsPublishers Spectrum Maths – Number: Teacher's Book 3

Main activity

▲ Construct a tally chart to show how many times each of the five vowels occur in this list of names.
▲ Draw a bar chart to illustrate the data in the tally chart.
▲ Compare results with previous estimates.

Developments

▲ Make a list of the first names of all the children in the class. Construct a tally chart to show how many times each vowel occurs. Draw a bar chart to illustrate the results. How does it compare with the previous chart?
▲ Collect the names of children in another class. How do the two classes compare?
▲ Investigate the frequency of occurrence of consonants.
▲ Extend to vowels in place names, e.g. Brighton, Sheffield, London.

Individual practice in Pupil Book 3
Activity 20 Vowels bar chart

Names and vowels

Complete the tally chart to show how many vowels are in each name.

Gary	Sean	Nicola
Tracey	Derek	Mandy
Kirsty	Lulu	Hari
Balarama	Dean	Kelly
Melanie	Pushpa	Donna
Nathan	Sally	Susan
Terry	Elizabeth	

vowel	tally	frequency
a		
e		
i		
o		
u		

Now draw a bar chart to show the frequency of the vowels.

frequency of vowels

frequency

20
19
18
17
16
15
14
13
12
11
10
9
8
7
6
5
4
3
2
1

a e i o u

vowels

21

Activity

Choosy game

Key vocabulary

total
straight line

Objectives

Understanding addition and subtraction
▲ Extend understanding of addition and recognise that it can be done in any order

Rapid recall of addition/subtraction facts
▲ Know by heart addition facts for numbers to 20

Introducing the activity

▲ Using number cards (1–10), select three cards, e.g. 4, 7, 2. Discuss different possible totals when selecting two of the cards, e.g. 4 and 7 make 11, 4 and 2 make 6, and 7 and 2 make 9.

▲ Extend this for different sets of three cards. What is the smallest/largest possible total each time?

Main activity

▲ Children play the game in pairs. Explain the rules:
  • Shuffle each set of cards and make three piles, face up.
  • Players take turns to select any two of the three cards showing, which have a total to match a number on the board.
  • A counter is then placed on the matching board number. The used cards are placed at the bottom of the piles.
  • Counters cannot be placed on a square that already contains a counter.
  • The winner is the first player to have four counters in any straight line.

Developments

▲ Extend to ten turns each. The winner is the player who places most counters.
▲ Use only two sets of cards in two piles.
▲ Extend the game to using cards 10–20. Discuss the different possible totals, i.e. 20–40. Create a board with these totals, then play the game.
▲ Invent a game which is based on the *difference* between the numbers on a pair of cards, instead of the total.

Materials

▲ Three sets of number cards (1–10)
▲ A set of counters for each player, all in one colour

<hr>

Individual practice in Pupil Book 3
Activity 21 Choosing numbers

Choosy game

21
Activity

You will need:
three sets of number cards (1–10)
a set of counters each

11	8	20	7	3	14
10	2	13	10	11	19
15	6	12	13	12	9
12	7	8	16	4	5
5	14	9	8	18	17
9	9	6	4	15	11
16	11	10	17	10	7

Making totals

Key
vocabulary

total

largest/
smallest

pair

Objectives

Understanding addition and subtraction
▲ Add three or four single-digit numbers mentally

Rapid recall of addition/subtraction facts
▲ Know by heart addition facts for numbers to 20

Reasoning about numbers
▲ Solve number problems and recognise simple patterns

Introducing the activity

▲ Using number cards (1–20), shuffle them and deal them out in five pairs. State the totals of each. Which pair has the smallest total? the largest? What is the largest possible total? (20 + 19 = 39) What is the smallest? (1 + 2 = 3)

▲ Extend this activity by shuffling the cards and dealing out three sets of three. Explore the totals.

Answers

For a total of 20, check children's answers.
Total 15:

2 cards	3 cards	4 cards	5 cards
1, 14	1, 2, 12	1, 2, 3, 9	1, 2, 3, 4, 5
2, 13	1, 3, 11	1, 2, 4, 8	
3, 12	1, 4, 10	1, 2, 5, 7	
4, 11	1, 5, 9	1, 3, 4, 7	
5, 10	1, 6, 8	1, 3, 5, 6	
6, 9	2, 3, 10	2, 3, 4, 6	
7, 8	2, 4, 9		
	2, 5, 8		
	2, 6, 7		
	3, 4, 8		
	3, 5, 7		
	4, 5, 6		

Main activity

▲ Encourage a systematic approach to exploring totals which make 20. Start by finding all the different ways of making 20 with two cards, then move on to three cards, and so on. Then search for different ways of making the total 20 using each card once only.

Developments

▲ Investigate how many different 2-card totals of 15 and 20 are possible.

▲ What is the maximum number of cards which make a total of 15? 20?

▲ Choose a total, e.g. 12. Investigate how many different 4-card totals you can find which make it.

▲ Change the set of cards from 1–20 to 5–25, for example.

Materials

▲ Number cards (1–20)

Individual practice in Pupil Book 3
Activity 22 Totals

Making totals

You will need: a set of number cards (1–20)

Here are three ways of making
the total 20.

Each card has been used only once.

$\boxed{9} + \boxed{11} = \boxed{20}$ 2 cards

$\boxed{5} + \boxed{7} + \boxed{8} = \boxed{20}$ 3 cards

$\boxed{10} + \boxed{6} + \boxed{3} + \boxed{1} = \boxed{20}$ 4 cards

Now try making the total 20 in other ways.

Now make the total 15 in different ways.

Now choose your own totals and make them with the cards.

23

Activity

Birthdays

Key vocabulary

Sunday...
Saturday

tally chart

bar chart

Objectives

Organising and using data

▲ Organise data in a simple frequency table

▲ Represent and interpret data in a bar chart

Introducing the activity

▲ Discuss the children's birthdays. Do they know if their birthday this year falls on a Saturday? a Wednesday...?

▲ Use a calendar to find the day of the week for each pupil's birthday. Ideally, provide each child with a copy of the calendar for the year, so that they can highlight their birthday.

▲ Make a list of the children on the board and write the day of their birthday alongside each name. Discuss what the data shows. Do some days occur more often than others?

Main activity

▲ The children complete the tally chart on the sheet, using the data collected on the board. They then draw a bar chart to represent the results.

▲ Ask questions to help them interpret the bar chart, such as:
  • How many birthdays are on Wednesday?
  • How many birthdays are on weekends? weekdays?
  • Which day of the week has the most/fewest birthdays?
  • How many more birthdays fall on Mondays than Thursdays?
  • How many fewer birthdays fall on Fridays than Sundays?
  • On which days do more than five of our birthdays fall? less than three?
  • How many other children have a birthday on the same day of the week as you?

Developments

▲ Collect similar data from another class, draw the tally chart, then the bar chart. Compare the two sets of data. Then combine the two sets of data.

▲ Collect and analyse data based not on the day, but the month of the children's birthdays.

Materials

▲ A calendar

▲ A list of the children's birthdays

Individual practice in Pupil Book 3
Activity 23 Birthday chart

Birthdays

birthday	tally	frequency
Sunday		
Monday		
Tuesday		
Wednesday		
Thursday		
Friday		
Saturday		

Days of birthdays

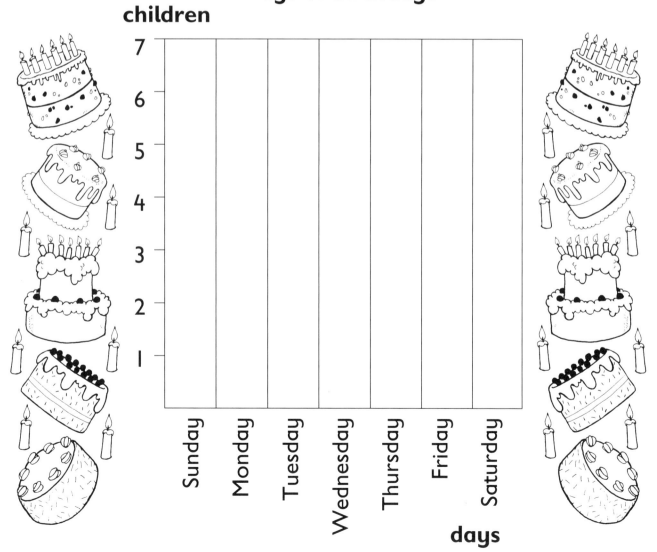

In between

Key vocabulary

difference
between
more/less
total
largest/
smallest

Objectives

Place value and ordering
▲ Use the vocabulary of comparing numbers

Understanding addition and subtraction
▲ Understand the operation of subtraction and the associated vocabulary

Rapid recall of addition/subtraction facts
▲ Know by heart subtraction facts for all numbers to 20

Mental calculation strategies (subtraction)
▲ Find a small difference by counting up from the smaller number to the larger

Introducing the activity

▲ Rehearse the concept of difference using number cards 11–20. Shuffle them and deal out two cards. Find the difference between the two numbers. Use the method of counting on from the smaller to the larger. Use a 1–20 number line to illustrate this. Repeat for different pairs of numbers.

▲ Deal out three cards, and put them in order from smallest to largest. Discuss which number is 'between' the other two. Find the differences between this number and both the smaller and the larger number. Repeat this activity for different sets of three cards.

Main activity

▲ Children play the game in threes. Explain the rules:
  • Each player shuffles a set of cards (11–20), and creates a pile, face down.
  • In round 1, each player reveals their top card. The player with the 'between' number scores zero points. The player with the largest number scores the difference between this and the 'between' number. Similarly, the player with the smallest number scores the difference between this and the 'between' number. If any players tie, all the players score zero.

  For example, if Player A's card is 13, B's is 17, and C's is 19, then:

    B scores 0 points, because 17 is the 'between' number
    A scores 4 points – the difference between 13 and 17
    C scores 2 points – the difference between 19 and 17.

  • Each player writes their scores on the score sheet.
  • In round 2, the next card on each pile is revealed, and so on.
  • The winner is the player with the highest total score after ten rounds.

Developments

▲ Use cards numbered differently, e.g. 1–20, 5–15, 10–30.
▲ The winner is the player with the lowest score after ten rounds.

Materials

▲ One set of number cards (11–20) for each player
▲ Sets of cards numbered differently
   (e.g. 1–20, 5–15, 10–30)

> **Individual practice in Pupil Book 3**
> Activity 24 Pairs differences

In between

24
Activity

You will need: three sets of number cards (11–20)

round	game 1 players		
	A	B	C
1			
2			
3			
4			
5			
6			
7			
8			
9			
10			
totals			

round	game 2 players		
	A	B	C
1			
2			
3			
4			
5			
6			
7			
8			
9			
10			
totals			

round	game 3 players		
	A	B	C
1			
2			
3			
4			
5			
6			
7			
8			
9			
10			
totals			

round	game 4 players		
	A	B	C
1			
2			
3			
4			
5			
6			
7			
8			
9			
10			
totals			

Asking questions

Key vocabulary

add

subtract

multiply

divide

fraction

question/ answer

half/double

Objectives

Rapid recall of addition/subtraction facts

▲ Know by heart addition and subtraction facts for all numbers to 20

Rapid recall of multiplication and division facts

▲ Know the 2 and 5 times-tables and begin to know the 3 and 4 times-tables

▲ Know doubles of numbers to 10 and corresponding halves

Fractions

▲ Recognise and find simple fractions of numbers

Checking results

▲ Check subtraction with addition, halving with doubling and division with multiplication

▲ Repeat addition or multiplication in a different order, or check with an equivalent calculation

Making decisions

▲ Choose appropriate operations to solve problems

Introducing the activity

▲ Look at the sheet and discuss the different calculations which have an answer of 8. Consider different additions, i.e. 0 + 8, 1 + 7, 2 + 6, 3 + 5... Discuss whether 5 + 3 is the same as 3 + 5. Extend this to additions involving three numbers, e.g. 1 + 2 + 5.

▲ Extend further to subtraction, then multiplication, then division. Include discussion about fractions, e.g. halving.

Main activity

▲ Children can approach the problem systematically by first only considering questions involving addition. These can be separated into addition of two numbers, then addition of more than two numbers, for example:

6 = 1 + 5, 2 + 4, 3 + 3

6 = 1 + 1 + 4, 1 + 2 + 3, 2 + 2 + 2

6 = 1 + 1 + 1 + 3, 1 + 1 + 2 + 2

6 = 1 + 1 + 1 + 1 + 2, 1 + 1 + 1 + 1 + 1 + 1

▲ Next, consider subtraction, then multiplication, and so on.

▲ Encourage the children to check their results, e.g. with an equivalent calculation or the inverse operation.

Developments

▲ How many different questions are possible, using '+' signs only?

▲ Try restricting the questions only to those which involve addition and subtraction.

▲ Try to create problems which have a given answer, e.g. I had four marbles, then I found two more. How many have I got altogether now?

Individual practice in Pupil Book 3
Activity 25 Making 10 and 12

Asking questions

The answer is $\boxed{8}$  | 5 + 3 = ? |

Here are some questions.

| 7 + 1 = ? |

| 10 – 2 = ? |

| 2 × 4 = ? |

| 2 + 3 + 3 = ? |

| half of 16 = ? |

| double 4 = ? |

Now write some different questions for an answer of $\boxed{6}$

Choose your own answers and write some
questions to match them.

Number cross

Objectives

Understanding multiplication and division
▲ Understand multiplication as repeated addition and that multiplication can be done in any order

Rapid recall of multiplication facts
▲ Know facts for the 2 and 5 times-tables and begin to know facts for the 3 and 4 times-tables

Reasoning about numbers
▲ Solve number problems

Introducing the activity

▲ Rehearse the concept of multiplication as an array, using counters or pegboards. Ask the children to take 12 counters, for example. Experiment with different ways of placing the twelve counters into rectangular arrangements, e.g. 1 × 12, 2 × 6, 3 × 4. Record these using the notation described on the sheet.

▲ Use a 'window' through which two squares on the cross can be seen. Place the window over different places randomly on the cross, e.g. 2, 4 horizontally. The children multiply the two numbers together, using a 2 × 4 array of counters, if necessary. Repeat this for different positions of the window.

▲ Introduce the vocabulary of 'horizontal' and 'vertical'.

Answers

Check the children's answers.
These are some possibilities:

1. $\boxed{5\ 2}$ 10   2. $\boxed{\begin{array}{c}2\\3\end{array}}$ 6   3. $\boxed{3\ 4}$ 12   4. $\boxed{\begin{array}{c}4\\1\end{array}}$ 4   5. $\boxed{2\ 4}$ 8

6. $\boxed{\begin{array}{c}3\\5\end{array}}$ 15   7. $\boxed{3\ 5}$ 15   8. $\boxed{\begin{array}{c}2\\1\end{array}}$ 2   9. $\boxed{4\ 1}$ 4   10. $\boxed{\begin{array}{c}4\\4\end{array}}$ 16

11. $\boxed{4\ 5}$ 20   12. $\boxed{\begin{array}{c}5\\5\end{array}}$ 25   13. $\boxed{1\ 1}$ 1   14. $\boxed{\begin{array}{c}3\\3\end{array}}$ 9   15. $\boxed{3\ 1}$ 3

Main activity

▲ Before completing the sheet, discuss with the children the possibility of there being several pairs of numbers which have a given product.

Developments

▲ Investigate all the different horizontal pairs and their products. How many different products are available? Extend the same activity to the vertical pairs of numbers.

▲ The children draw their own number cross, write their own numbers up to 5, (or some more than 5, including 10). They then investigate different pairs of numbers and their products.

Materials

▲ Squared paper
▲ Counters or pegboards

Individual practice in Pupil Book 3
Activity 26 Counters multiplication
Activity 26b How many coins?

Number cross

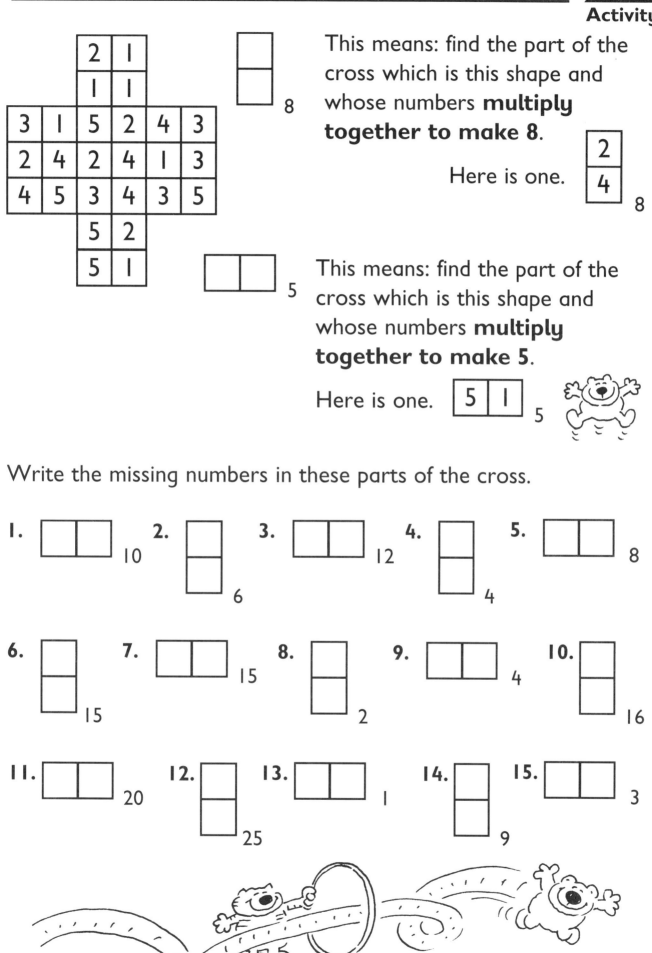

This means: find the part of the cross which is this shape and whose numbers **multiply together to make 8**.

Here is one.

2
4
8

This means: find the part of the cross which is this shape and whose numbers **multiply together to make 5**.

Here is one. | 5 | 1 | 5

Write the missing numbers in these parts of the cross.

1. ▢▢ 10   2. ▢/▢ 6   3. ▢▢ 12   4. ▢/▢ 4   5. ▢▢ 8

6. ▢/▢ 15   7. ▢▢ 15   8. ▢/▢ 2   9. ▢▢ 4   10. ▢/▢ 16

11. ▢▢ 20   12. ▢/▢ 25   13. ▢▢ 1   14. ▢/▢ 9   15. ▢▢ 3

27 Activity

Measuring game

Key vocabulary

measure
length
centimetre
nearest
centimetre
distance

Objectives

Measures

▲ Begin to write the vocabulary related to length
▲ Measure and compare to the nearest whole or half centimetre, using a ruler
▲ Estimate and record measurements to the nearest centimetre or half centimetre

Introducing the activity

▲ Throw a pair of dice and note the numbers, e.g. 1 and 5. Look at the sheet, and locate a 1-flag and a 5-flag. Emphasise that the activity focuses on the distance between the *bases* of the two flags. Ask the children to estimate the distance in centimetres, then to measure it with a ruler.
▲ Clarify what happens when the measure is not exact. Record the length to the nearest centimetre or half centimetre.

Main activity

▲ Children play the game in pairs. Explain the rules:
  • Players take turns to throw the two dice.
  • If a 5 and a 2 are thrown by Player A, for example, then a straight line should be drawn joining the base of a 5-flag and a 2-flag.
  • Player A then measures the line to the nearest whole or half centimetre. This is his/her score.
  • Once two flags are joined, they cannot be joined again, but either can be joined to a third point.
  • After five rounds, the winner is the player with the most points.

Developments

▲ Extend to playing ten rounds instead of five.
▲ The winner becomes the player with the fewest points.
▲ Investigate how many different scores are possible when joining two numbers.
▲ Take turns to throw three dice and draw a triangle joining the points. Score according to the length of the perimeter of the triangle.
▲ The children create their own sheet, marking their own points and flags, then play the game.
▲ Extend to measuring the length in centimetres *and* millimetres, and scoring the number of extra millimetres beyond the whole number of centimetres.
▲ Measure the length in centimetres and millimetres, and record in decimal notation.

Materials

▲ Two dice per game
▲ Rulers graded in centimetres and millimetres

Individual practice in Pupil Book 3
Activity 27 Measuring lengths

Measuring game

You will need: two dice

4

2

1

5

5

4

1

6

4

6

3

3

2

Activity **28**

Six additions game

Key vocabulary

total

addition

Objectives

Understanding addition and subtraction
▲ Add several single-digit numbers mentally

Rapid recall of addition/subtraction facts
▲ Know addition facts for numbers to 20

Mental calculation strategies (addition)
▲ Add three or four small numbers by putting the largest first or finding pairs totalling 9, 10 or 11

Introducing the activity

▲ Draw a copy of the score sheet on the board. Choose children to take turns to roll a dice and write the score in any one of the boxes (on the left-hand side of the equations). When the twelve boxes have been filled, discuss the six different totals, and write them in. Calculate the overall total of the six totals. Using counting on methods, find the totals of pairs of numbers first, then find the total of these numbers.

Main activity

▲ Children play the game in threes or fours, each with a score sheet.
Explain the rules:
  • One player throws the dice twelve times.
  • After each throw, all the players must write the number in one of their boxes, before the dice is thrown again. The object is to make additions with totals that appear more than once, i.e. sets of identical totals.
  • Once a number is written in a box, it cannot be changed.
  • When the twelve boxes have been completed, each player calculates their six totals. Any totals that appear only once are eliminated. The remaining totals are added together to give the player his/her score.
  • The winner is the player with the highest score.

Developments

▲ Investigate arrangements of the 12 numbers which will give the maximum score. Use number cards to help with this.
▲ Change the rules so that the winner is the player with the lowest score.
▲ Score all totals greater than 7, and eliminate all the others.
▲ Instead of using dice, use number cards (1–9) to generate the numbers for the additions.
▲ Create a similar game based on subtraction.

Materials

▲ One dice per game
▲ Number cards (1–9)

66

Individual practice in Pupil Book 3
Activity 28 Add them up

Six additions game

You will need: one dice

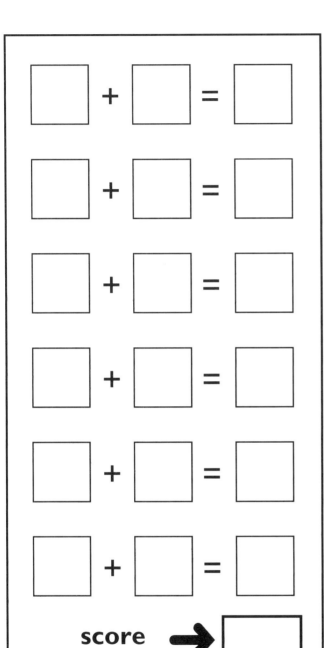

□ + □ = □

□ + □ = □

□ + □ = □

□ + □ = □

□ + □ = □

□ + □ = □

score ➡ □

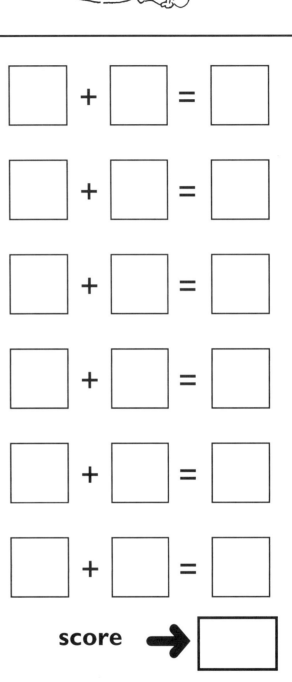

□ + □ = □

□ + □ = □

□ + □ = □

□ + □ = □

□ + □ = □

□ + □ = □

score ➡ □

Corner numbers

Key vocabulary

multiplying
dividing
triangle
square
pentagon
hexagon

Objectives

Counting and properties of numbers
▲ Recognise 2-digit multiples of 2, 5 or 10

Understanding multiplication and division
▲ Understand the concept of multiplication as repeated addition
▲ Understand that division is the inverse of multiplication

Rapid recall of multiplication and division facts
▲ Know multiplication facts for the 5 and 10 times-tables and begin to know facts for the 3 and 4 times-tables
▲ Derive division facts corresponding to the 3, 4, 5 and 6 times-tables

Mental calculation strategies (division)
▲ Use known number facts to divide by 3, 4, 5 and 6

Introducing the activity

▲ Consolidate multiplication as repeated addition. For example, consider 3 × 4 by adding three fours, e.g. 4 + 4 + 4 = 12. This can be illustrated using number rods, or rods of interlocking cubes.
▲ Extend by adding other sets of three like numbers.
▲ Develop towards linking multiplication to division, i.e. How can we make 15 by adding three like numbers?

Main activity

▲ Clarify the number of corners (vertices) for each of the shapes: triangles, squares, pentagons and hexagons.
▲ After completing the sheet, the children can write out the 3, 4, 5 and 6 times-tables and use these to check their answers.

Developments

▲ The children construct their own shapes with inside numbers.
▲ Investigate the different possible inside numbers for triangles, squares...
▲ Ask: What are the corner numbers on each shape if the inside number is 1? This will help to consolidate the concept of fractions.

Answers

Corner numbers

The number in the middle of the shape is the total of the numbers in the corners.
For each shape the corner numbers must be the same.
Write in the missing corner numbers.

1. 2 / 6 / 2 2
2. 6 / 18 / 6 6
3. 10 / 30 / 10 10

4. 4 / 12 / 4 4
5. 9 / 27 / 9 9
6. 12 / 36 / 12 12

7. 4 4 / 16 / 4 4
8. 6 6 / 24 / 6 6
9. 12 12 / 48 / 12 12

Write the corner numbers for shapes with these inside numbers.

10. triangles   15 (5) 21 (7) 3 (1) 33 (11) 90 (30) 24 (8)

11. squares   4 (1) 28 (7) 36 (9) 20 (5) 40 (10) 100 (25)

12. pentagons   20 (4) 35 (7) 15 (3) 40 (8) 10 (2) 55 (11)

13. hexagons   12 (2) 30 (5) 18 (3) 6 (1) 54 (9) 60 (10)

Materials

▲ Number rods, or interlocking cubes

Individual practice in Pupil Book 3
Activity 29 Dividing
Activity 29b Bags of money

Corner numbers

The number in the middle of the shape is the total
of the numbers in the corners.
For each shape the corner numbers must be the same.
Write in the missing corner numbers.

1.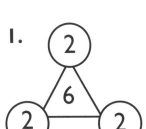
2.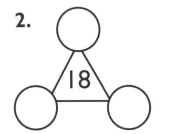
3.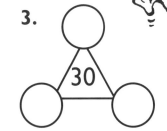

4.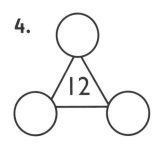
5.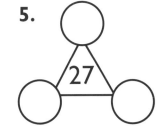
6.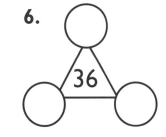

7.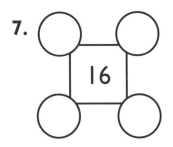
8.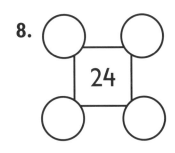
9.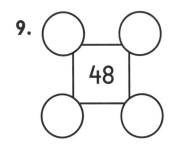

Write the corner numbers for shapes with these inside numbers.

10. triangles   15 ◯ 21 ◯ 3 ◯ 33 ◯ 90 ◯ 24 ◯

11. squares   4 ◯ 28 ◯ 36 ◯ 20 ◯ 40 ◯ 100 ◯

12. pentagons   20 ◯ 35 ◯ 15 ◯ 40 ◯ 10 ◯ 55 ◯

13. hexagons   12 ◯ 30 ◯ 18 ◯ 6 ◯ 54 ◯ 60 ◯

Triplets

Key vocabulary

total

Objectives

Understanding addition and subtraction
▲ Continue to recognise that addition can be done in any order and add three single-digit numbers mentally

Rapid recall of addition/subtraction facts
▲ Know addition facts for numbers to 15

Reasoning about numbers
▲ Solve number problems, working systematically, and recognise simple patterns

Introducing the activity

▲ Using a set of number cards (1–10), shuffle them and deal out three. Discuss methods of adding three numbers, e.g. starting with the largest, then adding the next largest, and finally add the third number to the total. Repeat for different sets of three cards.

Answers

For a total of 15, there are 10 different triplets.

1	4	10
1	5	9
1	6	8
2	3	10
2	4	9
2	5	8
2	6	7
3	4	8
3	5	7
4	5	6

For a total of 12, there are 7 different triplets.

1	2	9
1	3	8
1	4	7
1	5	6
2	3	7
2	4	6
3	4	5

Main activity

▲ Encourage the children to work systematically. For example, when finding triplets which total 15, one approach is to start with card number 1, then find all the pairs of numbers that total 14, to go with this. Then start with card number 2 and look for pairs which total 13, and so on.

Developments

▲ Try different totals for triplets. Start with the smallest possible total, i.e. 6 = 1 + 2 + 3, then try a total of 7, and so on. Is there any pattern?
▲ Try making quadruples, i.e. sets of four cards which have a given total.
▲ Try changing the range of cards available, e.g. 1–15, 5–20.

Materials

▲ Sets of number cards (1–10 and 1–20)

Individual practice in Pupil Book 3
Activity 30 Rows and columns

Triplets

You will need:
a set of number cards (1–10)

These three triplets total 15.

| 2 | 3 | 10 | | 3 | 4 | 8 | | 1 | 6 | 8 |

How many more can you find?

How many triplets can you find which total 12?

Choose your own total and find the triplets.

Car numbers

Objectives

Organising and using data
▲ Collect data in a tally chart/frequency table

Estimating and rounding
▲ Use the vocabulary of estimation, and begin to make sensible estimates

Introducing the activity

▲ Clarify the appropriate vocabulary, i.e. that 3, 7, and 9 are 'digits' and that 397 is a 3-digit number. Discuss how many digits there are (there are 10, from 0–9). Look at the sheet and discuss the position of the digits to avoid confusion between zero and the letter 'o'. Ask the children: Which digits do you think occur more often than others?... less often? How many car numbers are there altogether?

▲ Invite the children to estimate how many digits and 4s there are altogether.

Answers

digit	tally	frequency
0	III	3
1	I	1
2	III	3
3	IIII	4
4	HHT I	6
5	III	3
6	HHT III	8
7	HHT III	8
8	IIII	4
9	HHT	5

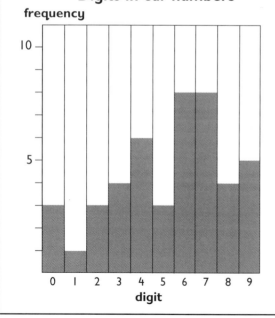

Digits in car numbers

Main activity

▲ Draw a tally chart to show the number of times each digit occurs.
▲ Draw a bar chart to illustrate the results of the tally chart.
▲ Ask questions to help the children interpret the results, such as:
  • How many 1s, 7s, 4s are there?
  • Which digit occurs 6 times? 4 times...?
  • Which digit occurs most often? least often?
  • Which is the most frequent odd digit? even digit?
  • How many more 7s are there than 4s?
  • How many less 2s than 6s?
▲ Compare the results with the children's estimates.

Developments

▲ Collect another set of fifteen car numbers from the school car park and/or cars passing on the road. Construct a tally chart, then draw the corresponding bar chart. Comment on the results. Compare the two bar charts.
▲ Analyse the letter frequency of the car registrations.

Materials

▲ Squared paper

Individual practice in Pupil Book 3
Activity 31 Tally chart
Activity 31b Goals tally

Car numbers

Finding totals

Objectives

Understanding addition and subtraction
▲ Extend understanding of the operation of addition and use the related vocabulary

Mental calculation strategies (addition)
▲ Put the larger number first and count on
▲ Partition into tens and units, then recombine
▲ Use known number facts and place value to add a single-digit number to a 2-digit number
▲ Bridge through a multiple of ten, then adjust

Reasoning about numbers
▲ Solve number problems, working systematically

Introducing the activity

▲ Use base ten material to consolidate the addition of a single-digit number to a 2-digit number. For example, for 24 + 5, i.e. an addition not crossing a 'ten', create the number 24 with the materials, then add five more units.

Answers

Altogether, there are three
different possible totals (from six
different arrangements).

24 + 5 = 29	45 + 2 = 47
25 + 4 = 29	52 + 4 = 56
42 + 5 = 47	54 + 2 = 56

Main activity

▲ Children need to record the results, whilst using the cards to create the different additions. Children can be encouraged to work systematically, by using one card as the single-digit number, then rearranging the other two cards to make two different 2-digit numbers. This creates two additions. Then another card can be chosen as the single-digit number, and so on.

Developments

▲ Try the activity with a different set of three number cards. Are there always three different totals possible?
▲ Try starting with four cards, and choosing three of them to create the addition. How many different totals are possible now?
▲ Extend to using four cards and adding two 2-digit numbers.
▲ Extend to subtracting a single-digit number from a 2-digit number.

Materials

▲ Base ten materials
▲ Number cards (1–9)

Individual practice in Pupil Book 3
Activity 32 Adding 2-digit numbers

Finding totals

You will need: these three number cards

The cards have been used to make a 2-digit number
and a single-digit number.

Then they have been added together.

$$\boxed{2}\,\boxed{4} + \boxed{5} = \bigcirc{29}$$

How many different possible totals can you find?

33 Activity

Equation people

Key vocabulary

addition
subtraction
equation

Objectives

Understanding addition and subtraction
▲ Continue to recognise that addition can be done in any order
▲ Extend understanding that subtraction is the inverse of addition

Rapid recall of addition/subtraction facts
▲ Know addition and subtraction facts for all numbers to 11

Understanding multiplication and division
▲ Recognise division as the inverse of multiplication

Checking results
▲ Check subtraction with addition and division with multiplication

Introducing the activity

▲ Use a number line (1–12) to illustrate the additions and subtractions. Alternatively, you might like to make a washing line with number cards pegged on the line. Highlight the cards 2, 5 and 7 using different coloured number cards, for example. Clarify that movements forwards along the line illustrate addition, and movements backwards illustrate subtraction. Show that 5 count on 2 makes 7, and that 2 count on 5 makes 7. Show also that 7 count back 2 makes 5, and 7 count back 5 makes 2.

Answers

1. 3 + 8 = 11
    8 + 3 = 11
    11 − 3 = 8
    11 − 8 = 3

2. 1 + 5 = 6
    5 + 1 = 6
    6 − 1 = 5
    6 − 5 = 1

3. 4 + 5 = 9
    5 + 4 = 9
    9 − 5 = 4
    9 − 4 = 5

    Questions 4–6 generate eight equations each.

Main activity

▲ Encourage the children to use number cards and mathematical sign cards (+, −, =) to generate the different equations.

Developments

▲ The children choose their own set of three numbers to write two additions and two subtractions.
▲ For the people with four numbers on their faces, investigate writing sentences using all four numbers, e.g. 8 + 2 = 4 + 6, or
    8 − 4 = 6 − 2.
▲ Extend to creating multiplications and divisions, e.g. 2, 4 and 8 leads to
    2 × 4 = 8, 8 ÷ 2 = 4, 8 ÷ 4 = 2.

Materials

▲ Number line (1–12) or 12 pegs on a 'washing line'
▲ Number cards (1–12)
▲ Mathematical sign cards (+, −, =, ×, ÷)

Individual practice in Pupil Book 3
Activity 33 Adding and subtracting

Equation people

Equation people live on the planet Equation.

They have three numbers on their faces which make two additions and two subtractions on their bodies.

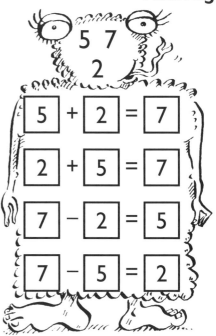

$5 + 2 = 7$

$2 + 5 = 7$

$7 - 2 = 5$

$7 - 5 = 2$

Complete the additions and subtractions for these equation people.

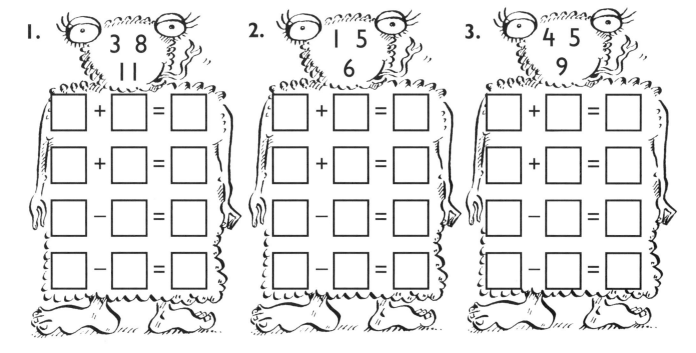

1. 3 8 11

☐ + ☐ = ☐

☐ + ☐ = ☐

☐ − ☐ = ☐

☐ − ☐ = ☐

2. 1 5 6

☐ + ☐ = ☐

☐ + ☐ = ☐

☐ − ☐ = ☐

☐ − ☐ = ☐

3. 4 5 9

☐ + ☐ = ☐

☐ + ☐ = ☐

☐ − ☐ = ☐

☐ − ☐ = ☐

These equation people have four numbers on their faces.
How many different additions and subtractions can you find for each person?

4. 8 6 2 4

5. 4 5 9 1

6. 3 7 10 4

Across and down puzzles

Objectives

Counting and properties of numbers
▲ Count on in steps of 3, 4, 5 from any small number

Understanding addition and subtraction
▲ Extend understanding of addition and subtraction

Rapid recall of addition/subtraction facts
▲ Know addition and subtraction facts for numbers to 20

Reasoning about numbers
▲ Solve a number puzzle, recognising patterns and relationships

Introducing the activity

▲ Using a number line (1–20), count on in steps of two, starting at different numbers. Extend this to counting on in steps of three, and so on. Record the sequences of numbers, both by writing the sequences horizontally, and by writing them vertically.

▲ Develop the recording of the sequences to include the method shown on the sheet, i.e. horizontally and vertically.

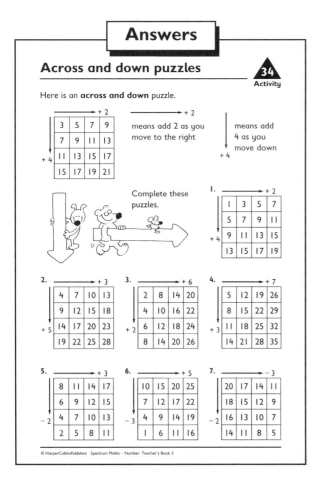

Main activity

▲ Encourage the children to use a number line or a 100 square to help them complete the sheet.

Developments

▲ Explore puzzles which have the number zero in the top left corner. Use this to search for relationships, i.e. for a +2 across and +3 down puzzle, then the top right square will be 3 × 2 = 6, and the bottom left will be 3 × 3 = 9. Also the largest number, in the bottom right, will be 3 × (2 + 3), i.e. 3 × 5 = 15.

▲ Invite children to try to predict the numbers in the top right, bottom left, and bottom right squares.

▲ Ask the children to devise their own similar puzzles.

▲ Extend to puzzles which are not square, i.e. 2 × 5 for example.

Materials

▲ Number line (1–20) or 100 square

Individual practice in Pupil Book 3
Activity 34 Additions
Activity 34b More additions

Across and down puzzles

Here is an **across and down** puzzle.

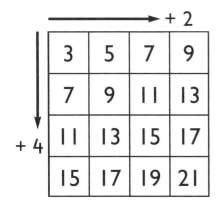

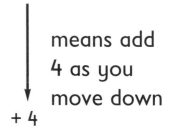

means add 2 as you move to the right

means add 4 as you move down

Complete these puzzles.

1.

→ + 2			
1	3	5	
5	7		
9			

+ 4

2. → + 3

4			

+ 5

3. → + 6

2			

+ 2

4. → + 7

5			

+ 3

5. → + 3

8			

− 2

6. → + 5

10			

− 3

7. → − 3

20			

− 2

Sorting numbers

35 Activity

Objectives

Counting and properties of numbers
▲ Recognise odd and even numbers

Place value and ordering
▲ Use the vocabulary of comparing and ordering numbers

Rapid recall of multiplication facts
▲ Know multiplication facts for the 5 times-table and begin to know the 3 and 4 times-tables

Reasoning about numbers
▲ Solve mathematical puzzles

Key vocabulary

row/column
more than/
less than
between
odd/even
multiple

Introducing the activity

▲ Using a number line (0–20), rehearse the vocabulary of comparing numbers, e.g. 'more than', 'less than', 'between', 'odd', 'even'. Recognise that 'more than 7', for example, does not include the number 7, and that 'between 5 and 8', for example, does not include 5 or 8.

▲ Use counting in steps of three, e.g. along the number line, starting at 0, to illustrate the multiples of three, i.e. the numbers in the 3 times-table. Extend to other multiples.

Answers

Sorting numbers — **35 Activity**

Sort the numbers on the balloons into the grids so they match both the row and column labels.

The first one has been done for you.

2.

Balloon: 2, 3, 1, 4

	odd	even
less than 3	1	2
more than 2	3	4

2.

Balloon: 4, 3, 6, 7

	less than 5	more than 5
odd	3	7
even	4	6

3.

Balloon: 12, 13, 11, 10

	less than 12	between 10 and 14
between 9 and 13	10	12
more than 10	11	13

4.

Balloon: 8, 6, 11, 9

	odd	even
less than 10	9	6
more than 6	11	8

5.

Balloon: 8, 6, 12, 15

	in the ×4 table	in the ×3 table
even	8	6
not less than 10	12	15

6.

Balloon: 5, 9, 15, 12

	in the ×3 table	in the ×5 table
more than 10	12	15
less than 10	9	5

7.

Balloon: 4, 5, 3, 1

	between 2 and 5	odd
between 3 and 8	4	5
less than 4	3	1

© HarperCollinsPublishers Spectrum Maths – Number: Teacher's Book 3

Main activity

▲ Ask the children to draw large versions of each grid on paper, then use number cards to match the numbers in the balloon. The numbers are then more easily sorted, and allow for freedom to experiment, before recording the results on the sheet.

▲ Explain to the children that, in some cases, a number can have more than one home, but that they should try to have one home for each number, rather than two numbers in one home, and none in another.

Developments

▲ For each sorting grid, use all the number cards 1–10, and find a home for each number. Extend this to numbers 1–20. How many numbers are in each 'home'?

▲ Ask the children to create their own sorting grid, using labels of 'more than' and 'less than' initially, and extending to include other labels.

Materials

▲ Number cards (0–20)
▲ Large sheets of paper and strips of card

Individual practice in Pupil Book 3
Activity 35 Sorting numbers

Sorting numbers

Sort the numbers on the balloons into the grids so they match both the row and column labels.

The first one has been done for you.

2.

Balloon: 2 3 1 4

	odd	even
less than 3	1	2
more than 2	3	4

2.

Balloon: 4 3 6 7

	less than 5	more than 5
odd		
even		

3.

Balloon: 12 13 11 10

	less than 12	between 10 and 14
between 9 and 13		
more than 10		

4.

Balloon: 8 6 11 9

	odd	even
less than 10		
more than 6		

5.

Balloon: 8 6 12 15

	in the ×4 table	in the ×3 table
even		
not less than 10		

6.

Balloon: 5 9 15 12

	in the ×3 table	in the ×5 table
more than 10		
less than 10		

7.

Balloon: 4 5 3 1

	between 2 and 5	odd
between 3 and 8		
less than 4		

Snake remainder game

Objectives

Understanding multiplication and division
▲ Begin to express a remainder as a whole number
▲ Recognise division as the inverse of multiplication

Rapid recall of multiplication and division facts
▲ Derive division facts for the 2, 3, 4, 5 and 6 times-tables

Mental calculation strategies (× and ÷)
▲ Say a division statement corresponding to a given multiplication statement

Introducing the activity

▲ Recall the multiplication facts for the 2 times-table, listing the multiples of 2. Extend to include the first five multiplication facts for the 3, 4, 5 and 6 times-tables.
▲ Rehearse the language of multiplication, e.g. 2 × 3 = 6 is read as 'two threes make six', and the language of division, e.g. the problem 6 ÷ 3 = ? can be presented as: How many threes make six?
▲ Illustrate the idea of a remainder, e.g. 5 ÷ 2 = ?, by asking: How many twos make five? And how many left over?

Main activity

▲ The children play the game in twos, threes or fours. Explain the rules:
  • Each player places a counter each at 'start'. They then take turns to throw both dice.
  • After each throw the number on the large dice is divided by the number on the small dice, to see if there is a remainder. If there is, the player moves his/her counter forward a number of spaces to match the remainder. If there is no remainder, the player does nothing.
  • The winner is the first to reach the head of the snake.

Developments

▲ Introduce a rule whereby the winning player must finish *exactly* on the last spot on the snake.
▲ Extend the divisions by using dice numbered differently, e.g. Write 12–17, or 18–23 on the larger dice.

Materials

▲ Dice (1–6), one per game
▲ Blank dice to make a 6–11 dice, one per game
▲ Counters

> **Individual practice in Pupil Book 3**
> Activity 36 Dividing machines
> Activity 36b More dividing

Snake remainder game

You will need: one dice (1–6)
one dice (6–11)
a counter each

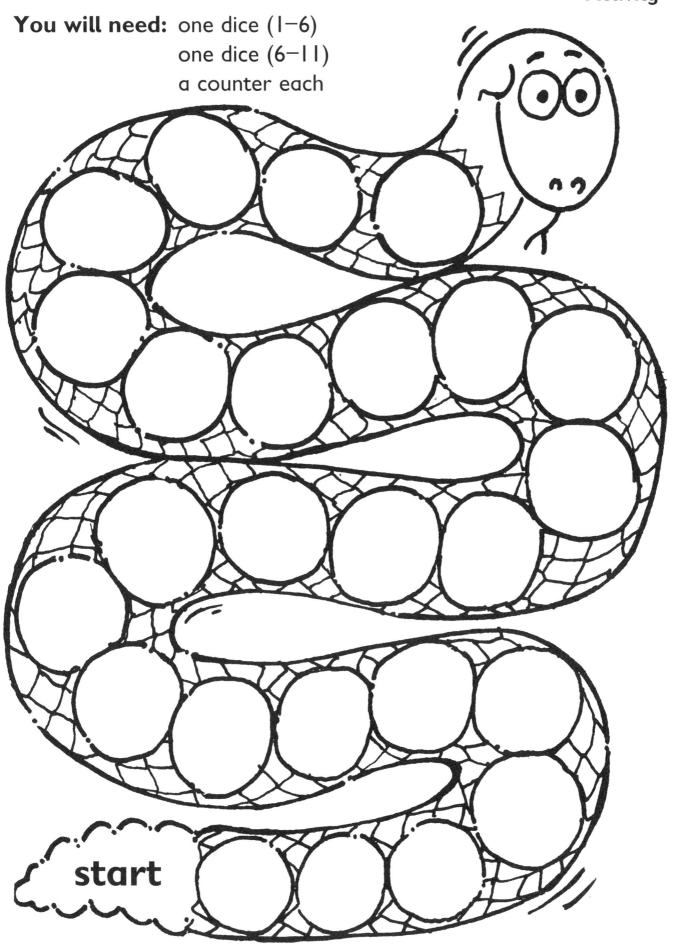

start

Digit sums

Activity 37

Key vocabulary

digit
square
diagonal

Objectives

Rapid recall of addition/subtraction facts
▲ Know addition facts for numbers to 20

Reasoning about numbers
▲ Recognise simple number patterns and relationships, generalise and predict

Introducing the activity

▲ Clarify the meaning of 'digit sum' in this context. This is straightforward when the total of the 2-digit number is less than 10. When it is greater than 10, then add the digits again to produce a single-digit answer. Practise finding digit sums of single-digit, 2-digit, and 3-digit numbers.

Answers

1	2	3	4	5	6	7	8	9	1
2	3	4	5	6	7	8	9	1	2
3	4	5	6	7	8	9	1	2	3
4	5	6	7	8	9	1	2	3	4
5	6	7	8	9	1	2	3	4	5
6	7	8	9	1	2	3	4	5	6
7	8	9	1	2	3	4	5	6	7
8	9	1	2	3	4	5	6	7	8
9	1	2	3	4	5	6	7	8	9
1	2	3	4	5	6	7	8	9	1

Main activity

▲ Give the children a 100 square each. Ensure they recognise that the entry on their blank square corresponds to the position of the number on the 100 square.
▲ Encourage the children to look for patterns, e.g. the sloping lines of like numbers. These could be coloured to highlight them.

Developments

▲ Explore numbers which have a digit sum of 9.
▲ Try extending the square beyond 100.
▲ Draw a similar square for the digit *difference*, instead of digit sum. Search for patterns.

Materials

▲ 100 squares
▲ Squared paper, preferably 1 cm square

Individual practice in Pupil Book 3
Activity 37 Digits

Digit sums

You will need: a 100 square

The digit sum of 13 is 4   add the digits 1 + 3 = 4

The digit sum of 57 is 3   add the digits 5 + 7 = 12

then add these new digits 1 + 2 = 3

Look at the 100 square. Work out the digit sum for each number. Write the digit sums on this blank 100 square.

When you have completed the square look for patterns.

38 Activity

Dice throwing

Key vocabulary

tally chart
bar chart
more/fewer

Objectives

Organising and using data
▲ Collect and record data in a tally chart/frequency table
▲ Represent and interpret data in a bar chart

Introducing the activity

▲ Discuss with the children what they think might happen when the dice is thrown several times. Do they think some numbers will show more often than others? Do they think that all numbers will show the same number of times? Try throwing the dice six times, and see what happens. Extend to throwing the dice twelve times.

Main activity

▲ Ask the children to record the 36 throws either by drawing the spots of the dice, or writing the number of spots.
▲ After recording the throws, children complete a tally chart to show how many times each number was thrown. Then they draw a bar chart to illustrate the results, for example:

score	tally	total
1	⊦⊦⊦⊦ 11	7
2	⊦⊦⊦⊦	5
3	⊦⊦⊦⊦ 1111	9
4	⊦⊦⊦⊦	5
5	1111	4
6	⊦⊦⊦⊦ 1	6
		36

scores on dice

▲ After completion of the sheet, ask questions to help the children interpret the results, such as:
 • How many throws scored 1? 2...?
 • Which score was thrown most often? least often?
 • Which scores were thrown more than six times? less than six times...?
 • How many more twos were thrown than fives?
 • How many fewer threes were thrown than fours?
 • How many throws scored more than 4, fewer than 3...?

Developments

▲ Repeat the experiment, again throwing the dice 36 times, and construct a second bar chart to illustrate the results. Compare the two sets of results.
▲ Try the experiment with a dice numbered differently, e.g. write 3, 4, 5, 6, 7, 8 on the faces of a cube.

Materials

▲ A dice (1–6)
▲ A blank cube

Individual practice in Pupil Book 3
Activity 38 Dice bar chart

Dice throwing

You will need: a dice (1–6)

Throw the dice 36 times. Record the score each time.

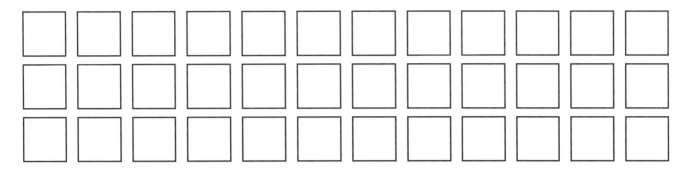

score	tally	frequency
1		
2		
3		
4		
5		
6		

Frequency of scores

frequency

14
13
12
11
10
9
8
7
6
5
4
3
2
1

1   2   3   4   5   6

score

Make the smallest

Objectives

Place value and ordering

▲ Know the value of each digit in a 3-digit number, and partition into hundreds, tens and ones (HTU)

▲ Compare 3-digit numbers, saying which is more or less

▲ Say the number which is 1, 10 or 100 more or less than any given 3-digit number

Reasoning about numbers

▲ Explain methods and reasoning about numbers

Introducing the activity

▲ Using number cards (0–9), shuffle the set of cards, and make three 3-digit numbers. Discuss which is the largest and which the smallest. Discuss the significance of looking at the first digit, i.e. the hundreds digit. Explain that if these are the same, then the tens digits should be compared.

▲ Practise creating 3-digit numbers based on the results of throwing a dice three times. Compare them and order them.

▲ Choose a given 3-digit number. Practise saying the number 1 more and 1 less, then 10 more and 10 less, and finally 100 more and 100 less.

Main activity

▲ Children play the game in twos, threes or fours, each with a score sheet. Explain the rules:
  • One player throws the dice four times. After each throw, all the players must:
    either write the digit in one of their boxes
    or say 'pass', and choose not to use the number.
    Encourage the children to explain their methods and reasoning.
  • Each player can only pass once.
  • Once a number is written in a box, it cannot be changed.
  • The aim is to make the smallest 3-digit number possible from the dice throws.
  • The player with the smallest number scores 2 points. The player with the next smallest number scores 1 point. Other players score 0 points.
  • After eight rounds, the winner is the player with the highest total score.

Developments

▲ Change the objective, e.g. aim to make the *largest* number.

▲ Throw three dice only, not allowing any passes.

▲ Throw five dice, and allow two passes.

▲ Instead of throwing a dice, use a shuffled set of number cards (0–9), to generate the three digits.

▲ Introduce a rule whereby the first number thrown cannot be placed in the hundreds place.

Materials

▲ Number cards (0–9)

▲ A dice (1–6)

> **Individual practice in Pupil Book 3**
> Activity 39 Abacus numbers

Make the smallest

You will need: a dice (1–6)

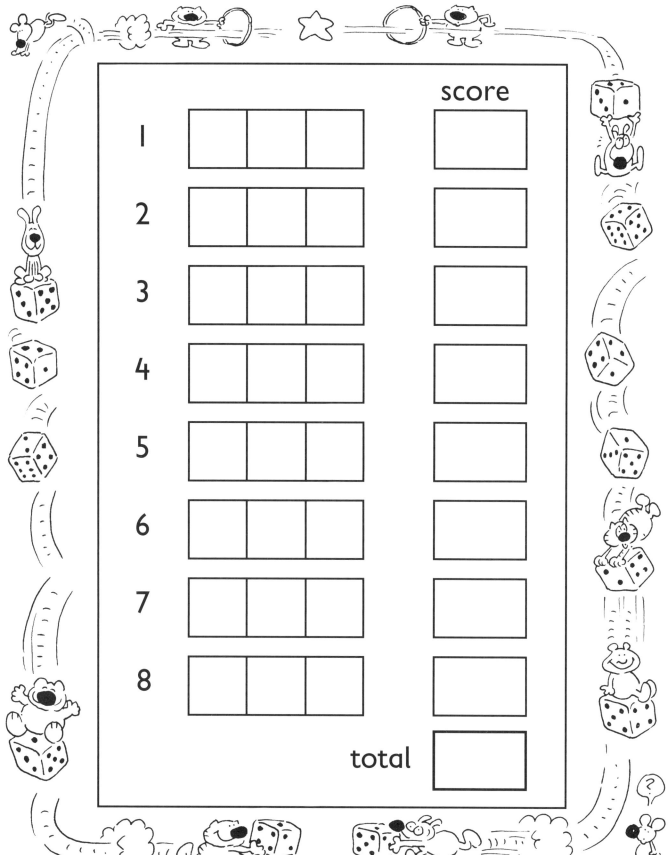

				score	
1					
2					
3					
4					
5					
6					
7					
8					
			total		

Dartboards

Activity

Objectives

Understanding addition and subtraction
▲ Add three or four single-digit numbers mentally, or 2-digit numbers with pencil and paper

Rapid recall of multiplication and division facts
▲ Know by heart doubles of numbers to 12 and doubles of multiples of 5 to 100

Reasoning about numbers
▲ Solve number problems or puzzles

Introducing the activity

▲ Use an enlarged copy of the dartboard photocopiable paper. Place a counter on different parts of the board, to help children to recognise the value of a dart in different positions.
▲ Rehearse doubling as repeated addition, e.g. double 6 is 6 + 6, or two sixes. Practise doubling numbers up to 12.

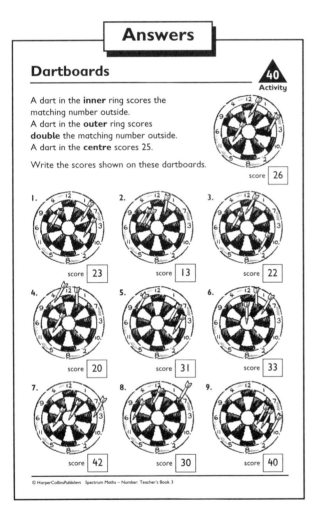

Main activity

▲ After completing the sheet, challenge the children to find different ways of making a total of 10 with three darts.

Developments

▲ Investigate different ways of making totals other than 12, with or without doubles.
▲ Use the dartboard paper to draw darts in different positions, and write the total scores.
▲ Investigate all the different possible scores with just one dart. Extend this to two darts, three darts…
▲ Children create their own dartboards, choosing their own numbers to place round the board. Choose, for example, multiples of 5.

Materials

▲ Dartboard paper (see photocopiable sheet on p.92)
▲ Counters

Individual practice in Pupil Book 3
Activity 40 Target doubles

Dartboards

A dart in the **inner** ring scores the matching number outside.
A dart in the **outer** ring scores **double** the matching number outside.
A dart in the **centre** scores 25.

Write the scores shown on these dartboards.

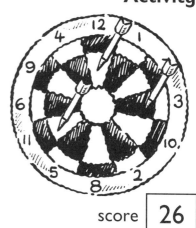

score | 26 |

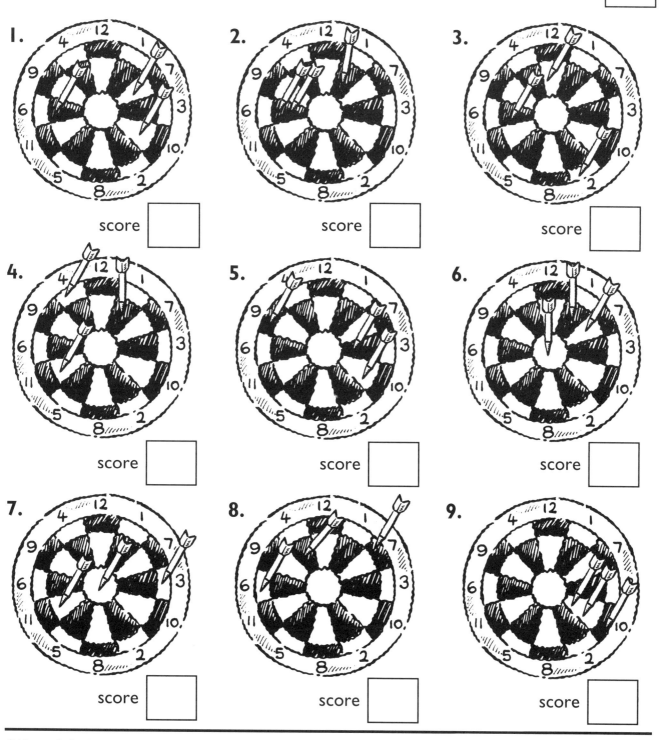

1.

score | |

2.

score | |

3.

score | |

4.

score | |

5.

score | |

6.

score | |

7.

score | |

8.

score | |

9.

score | |

Dartboard paper

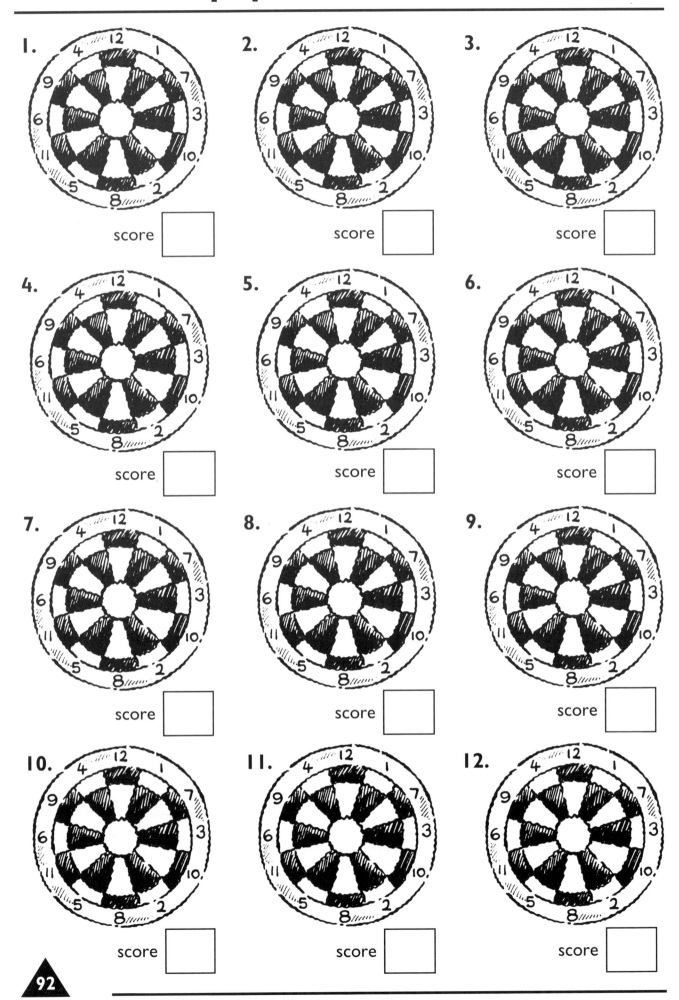

1.

score ☐

2.

score ☐

3.

score ☐

4.

score ☐

5.

score ☐

6.

score ☐

7.

score ☐

8.

score ☐

9.

score ☐

10.

score ☐

11.

score ☐

12.

score ☐

Pyramid paper

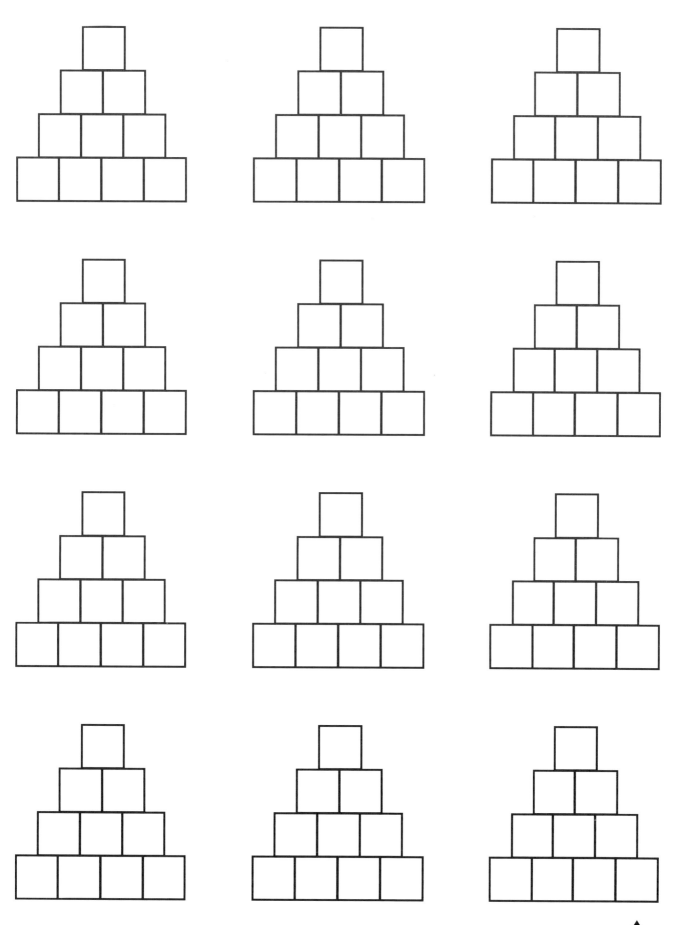

© HarperCollinsPublishers   Spectrum Maths – Number: Teacher's Book 3

Pupil book answers

Activity 1 3-digit numbers
1. 30   2. 200   3. 60   4. 500   5. 10
6. 300   7. 60   8. 5   9. 300
10. 132, 256, 347, 436, 512   11. 328, 509, 625, 743, 962
12. 304, 340, 343, 403, 430   13. 219, 237, 263, 274, 285
14. 347, 349, 350, 352, 358   15. 290, 299, 301, 310, 322

Activity 2 Missing numbers
1. $3 + 4 = 7$ 2. $5 + 5 = 10$
3. $6 + 8 = 14$ 4. $9 + 11 = 20$
5. $7 - 3 = 4$ 6. $10 - 6 = 4$
7. $18 - 6 = 12$ 8. $10 - 1 = 9$
9. $15 + 6 = 21$ 10. $12 + 11 = 23$
11. $4 + 2 + 4 = 10$ 12. $3 + 4 + 6 = 13$
13. $7 + 6 - 3 = 10$ 14. $5 - 2 + 9 = 12$
15. $6 + 3 - 4 = 5$ 16. $7 + 2 - 1 = 8$
17–22: Check the children's answers are correct.

Activity 3 Odds and evens
1. 475   2. 517   3. 315   4. 273   5. 247
6. 627   7. 543   8. 921   9. 601

1. 416   2. 168   3. 216   4. 260   5. 250
6. 276   7. 272   8. 390   9. 528

1. 235, 416, 475, 532   2. 168, 234, 349, 517
3. 207, 216, 315, 430   4. 260, 262, 270, 273
5. 219, 247, 250, 258   6. 267, 276, 627, 672
7. 272, 286, 491, 543   8. 390, 409, 512, 921
9. 463, 499, 528, 601

Activity 4 Multiplying
1. $2 \times 3 = 6$ 2. $1 \times 4 = 4$ 3. $2 \times 2 = 4$
4. $3 \times 5 = 15$ 5. $4 \times 3 = 12$ 6. $5 \times 2 = 10$
7. $4 \times 6 = 24$ 8. $6 \times 2 = 12$ 9. $6 \times 6 = 36$
10. $3 \times 4 = 12$ 11. $2 \times 5 = 10$ 12. $1 \times 6 = 6$
13. $2 \times 3 = 6$ 14. $3 \times 3 = 9$ 15. $2 \times 5 = 10$
16. $5 \times 5 = 25$ 17. $2 \times 4 = 8$ 18. $4 \times 4 = 16$

Activity 4b More multiplying
1. $3 \times 2 = 6$ 2. $1 \times 7 = 7$ 3. $5 \times 3 = 15$
4. $2 \times 5 = 10$ 5. $4 \times 4 = 16$ 6. $4 \times 2 = 8$
7. $6 \times 1 = 6$ 8. $3 \times 3 = 9$ 9. $3 \times 10 = 30$
10. $2 \times 5 = 10$ 11. $3 \times 4 = 12$ 12. $5 \times 3 = 15$
13. $4 \times 10 = 40$ 14. $6 \times 5 = 30$ 15. $1 \times 8 = 8$
16. $5 \times 5 = 25$ 17. $2 \times 7 = 14$

Activity 5 Reading a table
1. 3   2. 5   3. 6   4. 2   5. 4   6. 3
7. 4   8. 3   9. 4   10. 3   11. 3
12. Danni, Sean, Amit   13. Ruth

Activity 6 Adding three numbers
1. $4 + 2 + 1 = 7$ 2. $5 + 4 + 3 = 12$
3. $6 + 3 + 2 = 11$ 4. $7 + 3 + 4 = 14$
5. $5 + 6 + 2 = 13$ 6. $3 + 7 + 5 = 15$
7. $9 + 1 + 4 = 14$ 8. $5 + 3 + 7 = 15$
9. $3 + 1 + 2 = 6$ 10. $4 + 3 + 5 = 12$
11. $2 + 6 + 1 = 9$ 12. $4 + 5 + 2 = 11$
13. $3 + 3 + 3 = 9$ 14. $4 + 6 + 3 = 13$
15. $3 + 6 + 4 = 13$ 16. $7 + 3 + 5 = 15$
17. $2 + 8 + 7 = 17$

Activity 7 Adding
1. $1 + 3 = 4$ 2. $4 + 5 = 9$
3. $7 + 3 = 10$ 4. $2 + 8 + 3 = 13$
5. $4 + 7 + 6 = 17$ 6. $5 + 1 + 9 = 15$
7. $7 + 3 + 4 = 14$ 8. $1 + 5 + 9 = 15$
9. $5 + 7 + 5 = 17$ 10. $1 + 2 + 3 = 6$
11. $1 + 5 + 4 = 10$ 12. $1 + 2 + 6 = 9$
13. $4 + 3 + 5 = 12$ 14. $4 + 6 + 2 = 12$
15. $7 + 3 + 5 = 15$ 16. $3 + 1 + 2 + 4 = 10$
17. $1 + 2 + 5 + 6 = 14$ 18. $3 + 1 + 7 + 9 = 20$
19. $8 + 2 + 4 + 6 = 20$ 20. $3 + 8 + 1 + 9 = 21$
21. $3 + 7 + 4 + 9 = 23$

Activity 8 Differences
1. $d = 3$ 2. $d = 5$ 3. $d = 6$ 4. $d = 3$ 5. $d = 2$
6. $d = 6$ 7. $d = 5$ 8. $d = 5$ 9. $d = 6$
10. 8 or 2   11. 10 or 8   12. 10
13. 20 or 14   14. 25 or 9   15. 27 or 19
16. 36 or 32   17. 32 or 26   18. 47 or 33

Activity 9 Bar chart
1. 6 words   2. 6 words   3. 15 words   4. 2 words
5. 7 words   6. 4 words   7. 5 words   8. 8 words
9. 16 words   10. 24 words

Activity 10 Fractions
1. $\frac{1}{4}$ 2. $\frac{1}{3}$ 3. $\frac{1}{2}$ 4. $\frac{3}{4}$ 5. $\frac{2}{3}$
6. $\frac{1}{6}$ 7. $\frac{1}{10}$ 8. $\frac{3}{10}$ 9. $\frac{1}{8}$
$a = \frac{2}{10}$, $c = \frac{1}{5}$ $b = \frac{1}{2}$, $f = \frac{2}{4}$
$d = \frac{2}{8}$, $g = \frac{1}{4}$ $e = \frac{1}{3}$, $h = \frac{2}{6}$

Activity 11 Doubling
1. 6   2. 10   3. 8   4. 20   5. 14   6. 2
7. 24   8. 30   9. 22   10. 40   11. 80   12. 60
13. $8 + 3 = 11$ 14. $6 + 10 = 16$ 15. $5 + 18 = 23$
16. $12 + 7 = 19$ 17. $5 + 14 = 19$ 18. $12 + 14 = 26$
19. $40 + 25 = 65$ 20. $50 + 30 = 80$ 21. $60 + 30 = 90$

Activity 12 Balancing totals
1. 6   2. 5   3. 7   4. 7   5. 8
6. 6   7. 2   8. 3   9. 15
10. $3 + 4 = 1 + 6$ 11. $5 + 2 = 4 + 3$
12. $7 + 6 = 3 + 10$ 13. $8 + 2 = 4 + 6$
14. $6 + 5 = 7 + 4$ 15. $3 + 9 = 6 + 6$
16. $8 + 3 = 6 + 5$ 17. $9 + 1 = 3 + 7$

Activity 13 More differences
1. $d = 4$ 2. $d = 1$ 3. $d = 2$ 4. $d = 4$ 5. $d = 1$
6. $d = 3$ 7. $d = 0$ 8. $d = 3$ 9. $d = 1$ 10. $d = 4$
11. $d = 2$ 12. $d = 4$ 13. $d = 5$ 14. $d = 7$ 15. $d = 2$

Activity 14 Coin differences
1. $d = 1p$ 2. $d = 3p$ 3. $d = 9p$ 4. $d = 5p$
5. $d = 10p$ 6. $d = 15p$ 7. $d = 50p$ 8. $d = £1$
9. $d = 19p$ 10. $d = 2p$ 11. $d = 6p$ 12. $d = 3p$
13. $d = 5p$ 14. $d = 6p$ 15. $d = 9p$

Activity 15 More addition pyramids
1. 11 2. 11 3. 14 4. 14 5. 16 6. 17
7. 12 8. 15 9. 15 10. 4 11. 9 12. 5
13. 9 14. 8 15. 12 16. 5 17. 4 18. 15

Activity 16 5p, 10p, 20p coins
1. 20p 2. 30p 3. 30p 4. 35p 5. 30p
6. 25p 7. 65p 8. 40p 9. 50p
10. 20p, 10p, 5p 11. 20p, 5p, 5p 12. 10p, 5p, 5p
13. 20p, 20p, 10p 14. 20p, 10p, 10p 15. 10p, 10p, 5p
16. 20p, 20p, 5p

Activity 17 Next-door numbers
1. $3 + 4 = 7$ 2. $7 + 8 = 15$
3. $5 + 6 = 11$ 4. $11 + 12 = 23$
5. $15 + 16 = 31$ 6. $20 + 21 = 41$
7. $3 + 4 + 5 = 12$ 8. $6 + 7 + 8 = 21$
9. $4 + 5 = 9, 2 + 3 + 4 = 9$
10. $10 + 11 = 21, 6 + 7 + 8 = 21$
11. $7 + 8 = 15, 4 + 5 + 6 = 15$

Activity 18 3-card numbers
1. 873 2. 378 3. 738 4. 387 5. 873
6. 378 7. 378 8. 738 9. 387 10. 738
11. 146 12. 961 13. 146
14. 941 or 914 or 964 or 946 or 916 or 961
15. 461 or 469 16. 964 17. 614 or 619 18. 149
19. 496 20. 694

Activity 19 Taking away
1. $8 - 3 = 5$ 2. $5 - 1 = 4$ 3. $7 - 2 = 5$
4. $12 - 1 = 11$ 5. $15 - 3 = 12$ 6. $21 - 4 = 17$
7. $18 - 5 = 13$ 8. $14 - 2 = 12$ 9. $17 - 6 = 11$
10. 6 11. 13 12. 21 13. 14 14. 18
15. 27 16. 12 17. 7 18. 17
10. 2 11. 9 12. 17 13. 10 14. 14
15. 23 16. 8 17. 3 18. 13

Activity 20 Vowels bar chart
1. 11 2. 12 3. 5 4. 18 5. 9
6. i 7. o 8. a 9. u 10. e 11. u

Activity 21 Choosing numbers
1. $4 + 5 = 9$ 2. $7 + 4 = 11$ or $10 + 1 = 11$
3. $7 + 3 = 10$ 4. $10 + 7 + 5 = 22$
5. $5 - 1 = 4$ or $7 - 3 = 4$
6. $10 - 7 = 3$ or $7 - 4 = 3$ or $4 - 1 = 3$
7. $1 + 3 + 4 = 8$ 8. $10 + 5 + 4 = 19$
9. $6 + 2 = 8$ 10. $11 + 9 = 20$ 11. $2 + 8 = 10$
12. $13 + 6 = 19$ or $11 + 8 = 19$
13. $9 - 2 = 7$ or $13 - 6 = 7$
14. $13 - 11 = 2$ or $8 - 6 = 2$ or $11 - 9 = 2$
15. $2 + 6 + 11 = 19$ or $2 + 8 + 9 = 19$
16. $2 + 6 + 8 = 16$

Activity 22 Totals
1. $3 + 4 = 7$ 2. $5 + 6 = 11$
3. $7 + 2 + 1 = 10$ 4. $5 + 5 = 10$
5. $3 + 5 + 2 = 10$ 6. $10 + 13 = 23$
7. $3 + 2 + 5 + 1 = 11$ 8. $11 + 12 = 23$
9. $7 + 3 + 11 = 21$
10–18: Check the children's answers are correct.

Activity 23 Birthday chart
1. 3 2. 6 3. 5 4. 2 5. 4 6. 7
7. Friday 8. Wednesday 9. Monday
10. 3 more 11. 3 more

Activity 24 Pairs differences
1. $d = 7 - 2 = 5$ 2. $d = 5 - 4 = 1$
3. $d = 9 - 5 = 4$ 4. $d = 9 - 7 = 2$
5. $d = 4 - 2 = 2$ 6. $d = 9 - 2 = 7$
7. $d = 10 - 7 = 3$ 8. $d = 13 - 4 = 9$
9. $d = 18 - 15 = 3$ 10. $d = 15 - 10 = 5$
11. $d = 18 - 7 = 11$ 12. $d = 18 - 4 = 14$

Activity 25 Making 10 and 12
Check the children's answers are correct.

Activity 26 Counters multiplication
1. $2 \times 3 = 6$ 2. $4 \times 2 = 8$ 3. $3 \times 3 = 9$
4. $4 \times 3 = 12$ 5. $2 \times 5 = 10$ 6. $3 \times 1 = 3$
7. $2 \times 2 = 4$ 8. $4 \times 4 = 16$ 9. $5 \times 3 = 15$
10. $2 \times 4 = 8$ 11. $5 \times 2 = 10$ 12. $3 \times 4 = 12$
13. $1 \times 3 = 3$ 14. $3 \times 3 = 9$ 15. $4 \times 1 = 4$
16. $4 \times 3 = 12$ 17. $2 \times 5 = 10$ 18. $5 \times 5 = 25$

Activity 26b How many coins?
1. $4 \times 2p = 8p$ 2. $3 \times 2p = 6p$ 3. $7 \times 2p = 14p$
4. $2 \times 5p = 10p$ 5. $6 \times 5p = 30p$ 6. $3 \times 5p = 15p$
7. $5 \times 10p = 50p$ 8. $6 \times 10p = 60p$ 9. $3 \times 10p = 30p$
10. $4 \times 5p = 20p$ 11. $5 \times 5p = 25p$ 12. $8 \times 5p = 40p$
13. $7 \times 10p = 70p$ 14. $2 \times 10p = 20p$ 15. $8 \times 10p = 80p$

Activity 27 Measuring lengths
1. 8 cm 2. 5 cm 3. 4 cm 4. 3 cm 5. 6 cm
6. 11 cm 7. 7 cm 8. 10 cm 9. 9 cm 10. 7 cm
11. 11·5 cm 12. 10 cm 13. 17·5 cm 14. 6 cm 15. 8·5 cm

Activity 28 Add them up
1. $8 + 8 = 16$ 2. $9 + 8 = 17$
3. $6 + 9 = 15$ 4. $9 + 7 = 16$
5. $50 + 50 = 100$ 6. $30 + 50 = 80$
7. $40 + 60 = 100$ 8. $50 + 60 = 110$
9. $400 + 600 = 1000$ 10. $500 + 500 = 1000$
11. $600 + 600 = 1200$ 12. $300 + 500 = 800$

Activity 29 Dividing
1. $9 \div 3 = 3$ stamps 2. $15 \div 3 = 5$ stamps
3. $6 \div 3 = 2$ stamps 4. $27 \div 3 = 9$ stamps
5. $12 \div 3 = 4$ stamps 6. $30 \div 3 = 10$ stamps
7. $10 \div 5 = 2$ stamps 8. $25 \div 5 = 5$ stamps
9. $40 \div 5 = 8$ stamps 10. $15 \div 5 = 3$ stamps
11. $35 \div 5 = 7$ stamps 12. $50 \div 5 = 10$ stamps

Activity 29b Bags of money
1. $8 \div 2 = 4$ coins 2. $14 \div 2 = 7$ coins
3. $10 \div 2 = 5$ coins 4. $18 \div 2 = 9$ coins
5. $24 \div 2 = 12$ coins 6. $16 \div 2 = 8$ coins
7. $25 \div 5 = 5$ coins 8. $50 \div 5 = 10$ coins
9. $30 \div 5 = 6$ coins 10. $35 \div 5 = 7$ coins
11. $40 \div 5 = 8$ coins 12. $55 \div 5 = 11$ coins

Activity 30 Rows and columns
1. $3 + 2 + 1 = 6$ 2. $5 + 4 + 3 = 12$
3. $6 + 2 + 1 = 9$ 4. $3 + 1 + 3 = 7$
5. $4 + 2 + 5 = 11$ 6. $6 + 4 + 5 = 15$
7. $7 + 9 + 2 = 18$ 8. $3 + 1 + 6 = 10$
9. $4 + 8 + 5 = 17$ 10. $7 + 4 + 3 = 14$
11. $6 + 1 + 2 = 9$ 12. $8 + 5 + 9 = 22$
13. $7 + 3 + 4 = 14$ 14. $9 + 1 + 8 = 18$
15. $2 + 6 + 5 = 13$ 16. $7 + 6 + 8 = 21$
17. $4 + 1 + 5 = 10$ 18. $3 + 2 + 9 = 14$

Activity 31 Tally chart

digit	tally	frequency
0	HHT	5
1	HHT I	6
2	HHT IIII	9
3	HHT IIII	9
4	HHT II	7
5	HHT I	6
6	HHT	5
7	HHT III	8
8	III	3
9	HHT	5

Activity 31b Goals tally

goals	tally	total
0	HHT IIII	9
1	HHT HHT HHT I	16
2	HHT HHT I	11
3	HHT II	7
4	IIII	4
5	II	2
6	I	1

Activity 31b continued
1. 7   2. 16   3. 9   4. 1   5. 4
6. 11   7. 7   8. 25   9. 11   10. 25

Activity 32 Adding 2-digit numbers
1. $47 + 22 = 69$ 2. $35 + 24 = 59$ 3. $26 + 35 = 61$
4. $52 + 29 = 81$ 5. $36 + 45 = 81$ 6. $64 + 23 = 87$
7. $55 + 26 = 81$ 8. $18 + 27 = 45$ 9. $29 + 32 = 61$
10. $54 + 23 = 77$ or $53 + 24 = 77$ or $45 + 32 = 77$
or $42 + 35 = 77$ 11. $57 + 41 = 98$ or $47 + 51 = 98$
12. $26 + 53 = 79$ or $23 + 56 = 79$
13. $47 + 21 = 68$ or $41 + 27 = 68$

Activity 33 Adding and subtracting
1. $4 + 3 = 7, 7 - 3 = 4, 7 - 4 = 3$
2. $5 + 4 = 9, 9 - 4 = 5, 9 - 5 = 4$
3. $8 + 3 = 11, 11 - 3 = 8, 11 - 8 = 3$
4. $6 + 9 = 15, 15 - 9 = 6, 15 - 6 = 9$
5. $5 + 12 = 17, 17 - 12 = 5, 17 - 5 = 12$
6. $19 + 11 = 30, 30 - 11 = 19, 30 - 19 = 11$
7. $2 + 6 = 8, 8 - 6 = 2$
8. $2 + 3 = 5, 5 - 3 = 2$
9. $1 + 5 = 6, 6 - 5 = 1$
10. $5 + 3 = 8, 8 - 3 = 5$
11. $14 + 5 = 19, 19 - 5 = 14$
12. $13 + 7 = 20, 20 - 7 = 13$

Activity 34 Additions
1a. $3 + 6 = 9$ b. $2 + 6 = 8$ c. $5 + 6 = 11$
d. $9 + 6 = 15$ e. $4 + 6 = 10$ f. $6 + 6 = 12$
g. $8 + 6 = 14$ h. $11 + 6 = 17$ i. $15 + 6 = 21$
j. $21 + 6 = 27$

2a. $3 + 9 = 12$ b. $2 + 9 = 11$ c. $5 + 9 = 14$
d. $9 + 9 = 18$ e. $4 + 9 = 13$ f. $6 + 9 = 15$
g. $8 + 9 = 17$ h. $11 + 9 = 20$ i. $15 + 9 = 24$
j. $21 + 9 = 30$

3a. $3 + 21 = 24$ b. $2 + 21 = 23$ c. $5 + 21 = 26$
d. $9 + 21 = 30$ e. $4 + 21 = 25$ f. $6 + 21 = 27$
g. $8 + 21 = 29$ h. $11 + 21 = 32$ i. $15 + 21 = 36$
j. $21 + 21 = 42$

4a. $6p + 2p = 8p$ b. $5p + 2p = 7p$
c. $14p + 2p = 16p$ d. $17p + 2p = 19p$
e. $40p + 2p = 42p$ f. $21p + 2p = 23p$
g. $60p + 2p = 62p$ h. $56p + 2p = 58p$

5a. $6p + 12p = 18p$ b. $5p + 12p = 17p$
c. $14p + 12p = 26p$ d. $17p + 12p = 29p$
e. $40p + 12p = 52p$ f. $21p + 12p = 33p$
g. $60p + 12p = 72p$ h. $56p + 12p = 68p$

Activity 34b More additions
1. $12 + 3 = 15$ 2. $15 + 4 = 19$ 3. $16 + 5 = 21$
4. $11 + 7 = 18$ 5. $17 + 5 = 22$ 6. $13 + 4 = 17$
7. $18 + 6 = 24$ 8. $10 + 9 = 19$ 9. $19 + 3 = 22$
10. $23 + 7 = 30$ 11. $27 + 4 = 31$ 12. $34 + 5 = 39$
13. $12 + 3 = 15$ 14. $15 + 4 = 19$ 15. $16 + 4 = 20$
16. $12 + 7 = 19$ 17. $13 + 6 = 19$ 18. $18 + 4 = 22$
19. $19 + 7 = 26$ 20. $13 + 9 = 22$ 21. $25 + 6 = 31$
22. $34 + 7 = 41$

Activity 35 Sorting numbers
1. 3, 5, 7, 9   2. 2, 6, 8   3. 5, 6, 7, 8
4. 2, 3, 5   5. 6, 7, 8, 9   6. 2, 6, 8
7. 3, 12, 15, 18, 21   8. 10, 12, 16, 18, 20
9. 5, 10, 15, 20   10. 10, 20
11. 10, 12   12. 3, 5, 7, 15, 21
13. 2, 4, 6, 8, 10, 12, 14   14. 3, 6, 9, 12, 15
15. 4, 8, 12   16. 5, 10, 15
17. 10   18. 6, 12

Activity 36 Dividing machines
1. $10 \div 5 = 2$ 2. $15 \div 5 = 3$ 3. $25 \div 5 = 5$
4. $40 \div 5 = 8$ 5. $20 \div 5 = 4$ 6. $5 \div 5 = 1$
7. $35 \div 5 = 7$ 8. $50 \div 5 = 10$ 9. $30 \div 5 = 6$
10. $45 \div 5 = 9$ 11. $11 \div 5 = 2$ r1   12. $23 \div 5 = 4$ r3
13. $8 \div 5 = 1$ r3   14. $14 \div 5 = 2$ r4   15. $31 \div 5 = 6$ r1
16. $52 \div 5 = 10$ r2   17. $9 \div 5 = 1$ r4   18. $16 \div 5 = 3$ r1
19. $25 \div 5 = 5$ r0   20. $36 \div 5 = 7$ r1

Activity 36b More dividing
1. $6 \div 2 = 3$ 2. $12 \div 3 = 4$ 3. $4 \div 4 = 1$
4. $20 \div 5 = 4$ 5. $30 \div 10 = 3$ 6. $10 \div 2 = 5$
7. $15 \div 5 = 3$ 8. $8 \div 4 = 2$ 9. $50 \div 10 = 5$
10. $9 \div 3 = 3$ 11. $14 \div 2 = 7$ 12. $5 \div 5 = 1$
13. $4 \div 2 = 2$ 14. $15 \div 5 = 3$ 15. $12 \div 3 = 4$
16. $40 \div 10 = 4$ 17. $18 \div 2 = 9$ 18. $20 \div 5 = 4$
19. $70 \div 10 = 7$ 20. $20 \div 4 = 5$ 21. $18 \div 9 = 2$
22. $7 \div 7 = 1$ 23. $100 \div 10 = 10$ 24. $22 \div 2 = 11$

Activity 37 Digits
Check the children's asnswers are correct.

Activity 38 Dice bar chart
1. 8   2. 3   3. 9   4. 4   5. 7   6. 6   7. 2
8. 4   9. 5   10. 5   11. 3   12. 3   13. 1

Activity 39 Abacus numbers
1. 231   2. 351   3. 463   4. 527   5. 345
6. 196   7. 285   8. 103   9. 506

in order: 103, 196, 231, 285, 345, 351, 463, 506, 527
For the second part of the activity, check the children's
answers are correct.

Activity 40 Target doubles
1. $5 + 40 + 10 = 55$ 2. $25 + 5 + 5 = 35$
3. $10 + 25 + 15 = 50$ 4. $60 + 20 + 10 = 90$
5. $120 + 10 + 5 = 135$ 6. $40 + 60 + 5 = 105$
7. $200 + 100 + 10 = 310$ 8. $100 + 80 + 10 = 190$
9. $160 + 10 + 5 = 175$

For the second part of the activity, check the children's
answers are correct.